In Seven Stages

In Seven Stages

A Flying Trap Around the World

Elizabeth Bisland

MINT EDITIONS

In Seven Stages: A Flying Trap Around the World was first published in 1891.

This edition published by Mint Editions 2021.

ISBN 9781513292236 | E-ISBN 9781513295084

Published by Mint Editions®

MINT EDITIONS

minteditionbooks.com

Publishing Director: Jennifer Newens
Design & Production: Rachel Lopez Metzger
Project Manager: Micaela Clark
Typesetting: Westchester Publishing Services

Contents

First Stage

If, on the 13th of November, 1889, some amateur prophet had foretold that I should spend Christmas Day of that year in the Indian Ocean, I hope I should not by any open and insulting incredulity have added new burdens to the trials of a hard-working soothsayer—I hope I should, with the gentleness due a severe case of aberrated predictiveness, have merely called his attention to that passage in the Koran in which it is written, "The Lord loveth a cheerful liar"—and bid him go in peace. Yet I did spend the 25th day of December steaming through the waters that wash the shores of the Indian Empire, and did do other things equally preposterous, of which I would not have believed myself capable if forewarned of them. I can only claim in excuse that these vagaries were unpremeditated, for the prophets neglected their opportunity and I received no augury.

On the 14th of November of the aforementioned year, I was awakened at eight o'clock as usual by the maid with the breakfast tray—which also contained the morning papers and a neat pile of notes and letters. Among these latter were acceptances of invitations I had sent to half a dozen agreeable folk to come and drink five-o'clock tea with me on the 15th, the usual communications from one's friends on casual subjects; an invitation to dinner; a bill; and a notice from my tailor that I might sometime during the day have the final fitting of a gown in process of construction. All as pleasantly commonplace as the most mild-mannered individual could expect or desire.

I read the papers leisurely, made a calm and uneventful toilet, and the very first intimation I received of the coming thunderbolt out of the serene sky of my existence was a hurried and mysterious request, at half-past ten o'clock, that I would come as soon as possible to the office of the magazine of which I was one of the editors. My appetite for mystery at that hour of the day is always lamentably feeble, and it was nearly eleven before I found time to go and investigate this one, although the office in question was only a few minutes' walk from my residence. On arriving, the editor and owner of the magazine asked if I would leave New York that evening for San Francisco and continue from there around the world, endeavoring to complete the journey in some absurdly inadequate space of time.

If my appetite for mystery at that hour is not strong, my appetite at eleven in the morning for even the most excruciatingly funny jokes may be said to actually not exist, and this one, I remember, bored me more than most. But in the course of half an hour I had become convinced that the editor really wished me to make the attempt, and I had earnestly endeavored to convince him that I meant to do nothing of the sort. To begin with, I didn't wish to. In the second place, guests were coming to my house to tea on the following day; thirdly, I was not prepared in the matter of appropriate garments for such an abrupt departure, and lastly, but most weightily, I foresaw the notoriety that an effort to outdo the feat of Jules Verne's hero was likely to bring upon me, and to this notoriety I most earnestly objected. Though for some years I had been more or less connected with journalism, I had appeared in the papers only as the contributor of unsigned articles, and the amount of distress I experienced when I first saw my name in a head line was so far beyond even my anticipations that I then and there registered a vow—Throughout this voyage I had cause to owe much gratitude to journalists for all manner of aid and civility, but I resolved in the future to so endeavor to conduct myself that they would never have reason to put my name in a head line again.

The editor and I having passed the better part of an hour going over this matter, substantial arguments were finally advanced by him which persuaded me to make the experiment of lowering the circumnavigatory record. I then took a cab and drove to my tailor for the appointed fitting and for a vigorous interview in which he was ultimately convinced that I *could* wear that gown at six o'clock in the evening.

The next few hours were busy ones.

To the masculine mind there appears to be something strangely exhilarating in the thought of a woman being abruptly torn from her home without sufficient time to put her wardrobe in order, and to all the men responsible for this voyage the most delightful feature apparently of the whole affair was the fact that I should be forced to get ready in five hours for a seventy-five days' voyage around the world.—Why this should be so a woman cannot easily divine. It fails utterly to appeal to *her* sense of humor. It is one of those hopeless warps in the male mind that my sex no longer attempt to comprehend or to straighten, and, finding it incurable, have learned to bear with and ignore it as far as possible.

I finally managed to get all absolute necessaries of travel into a good-sized steamer trunk, a large Gladstone bag and a shawl-strap, but found, by experience, that my progress would have been in no degree retarded, and my comfort and happiness far better served, by carrying a second and larger box with everything I could possibly have required. I managed the trip on two cloth gowns, half a dozen light bodices, and an evening silk, but might quite as well have carried my entire winter and a large part of my summer wardrobe. Happily I took the precaution of carrying plenty of pins and hair-pins. I had had some previous experience with their vicious ways, and well knew that in critical moments in foreign parts they would get up playful little games of hide-and-seek that would tend to undermine my temper, and the only sure preventive was to have geologic layers of them all through the trunk, so that a shaft might be hastily sunk through one's belongings at any moment with a serene certainty of striking rich deposits of both necessities of female existence.

. . . To wake up in the morning to one's usual daily duties and find one's self at night voyaging round the world is an experience calculated to surprise even a mind as composed as that of Pet Marjorie's historically placid fowl; and looking back now over the time of my departure I find that, though to outward seeming I also was

"*. . . most exceeding ca'm,*"

in reality I was practically stupefied with astonishment for at least two days.

I remember thinking rapidly on all manner of subjects; telling myself warningly that it would not do to forget anything or make any mistakes, as they could not be rectified. . . I remember thinking that my new gown fitted very well, and that, though my face was drawn and white with the excitement and fatigues of the day, my new hat was distinctly becoming. . . Then there were cabs and hurry—kisses—last directions—the bumping of the box on the stair—a big bunch of pink roses (which I felt was a nice complimentary touch to my travelling ensemble)—everybody talking at once and giving different advice and directions—the glare of lights—the coffin-like smell of a sleeping-car—and I was off for seventy-five days' travel round the globe.

. . . Then no more distinct impressions until Chicago suddenly steps across my twenty-five-thousand-mile path and it is necessary to change cars.

. . . Even this is vague. I remember that through some mistake there was no one there to meet me as had been arranged—that I wandered about a vast, gloomy, and rather empty station in the care of a friendly conductor—that I sat on a high stool at a counter and quenched internal cravings, caused by lack of dinner, with tea and ham; every mouthful regarded with wan interest by the person who officiated in the echoing lunch hall—that the conductor having bidden me a commiserating adieu, I slid away into the night, very homesick, very cross, and haunted by the bitterest suspicions of the happy results of a tea-and-ham dinner.

But with that night's sleep I slept away my stupefaction of amazement, and awoke at daybreak in my right mind, and, pulling up my window curtain, found the sun almost ready to rise.

I have never permitted a vulgar familiarity to dull my keen delight in the ever-varying pageant of the breaking of day; so that, consequently, on the rare occasions when I assist at this function, my pleasure has all the enthusiasm of novelty.

Now the lifted curtain showed me a New Jerusalem. . . As if to one who should rise to pray at the moment when God gave his great daily fiat of "Let there be light," there should be vouchsafed a white, luminous foreshadowing of that which it hath not entered into the heart of man to understand. . . Not the strangely narrow and urban vision of Patmos; no streets or walls, but a limitless Land of Pearl!

. . . Soft undulations, full and tender as the bosom of a sleeping mother, rose and fell far beyond the eye's reach, and melted into the sky. No tree or thicket broke the suave outlines, but where the thin silver veins of the streams slipped through the curves of the plain, slim, leafless willows hung, like glistening fringes. . . In the night a hoar frost had fallen that was to snow as sleep is to death; and the pale reaped fields, the sere meadows, and silent uplands were transfigured by the first gleam of day to a mystery and glory of silver and pearl. As the light grew, nacreous tints of milky blue and rose flushed the argent pallor of the land, and when the yellow disk rolled up over the horizon's edge I travelled for some brief space in a world of intolerable splendor, where innumerable billions of frost crystals flashed back to the sun the reflection of his shining face. Even the engine-driver was moved, I fancy, by this marvellous morning vision, for though we were far from any stopping-place, there suddenly thrilled through the silence a long, keen, triumphant blast, and we trailed as we flew floating golden plumes of steam. . .

As I passed in my swift circle about the great ball plunging along its planetary paths, many mighty and glorious visions of the coming and passing of light were revealed to me; but none more fair than this with that radiance of youth, whose vast, sweet nature-shadow and simulacrum the dawning is. . . Eternally renewed, through all ages. . . still, with the white peace of innocence. . . joyous in unwasted strength and untried powers. . . rosy with promise and potentialities, gilding all the commonplaceness of the landscape with golden glamours and fantasies. . . an Eden created out of the hollow void of night, in which to rest for one dewy, enchanted moment of purity and love before the sun with his flaming sword drives us forth to the toil and heat of the day!

. . . In developing my mental Kodak roll after returning, I found that during this period of the journey most of the views are landscapes, seeing that I was afflicted with peculiarly uninteresting fellow-travellers who made poor subjects for snap shots. Across the aisle from me was a pair of ancient little lovers who numbered some hundred or more years between them, I fancy. They had nested long since; all their fledglings were flown, and, left alone together once more, they were on their way to Los Angeles to spend a second honeymoon among the winter orange blossoms: a pretty pale afterglow of love. But though their quaint, antiquated billing and cooing was a pleasing enough thing to watch, it is notorious that even in these second bridal journeys the outsider is very much outside, and I was driven back perforce to my window.

. . . "A perfect day," the record says. . . More undulant fields clothed in the yellow stubble of the gathered harvest. Here and there black loam broken for winter sowing—a square of jet set in the pale amber— and over all a faint, turquoise sky. . .

That night we were in Council Bluffs, Omaha, and by chance got passage on the new fast mail-train, which had been put on as an experiment in time across the continent, and was carrying but one sleeper and the General Manager's private car.

The pace was tremendous from the start. . . We began to climb the Great Divide. Trees and shrubs grew rare and more rare, and finally vanished altogether.

. . . Great gray plains lay all about us, covered thinly with a withered, ashen-colored plant; the bitter results of an unequal struggle for existence, and strangely resembling in miniature the gnarled, writhen cedars that cling to wind-scourged coasts. Settlements were few and far between. Scrawny horses picked up a scant living in the desolate upland meadows; and an occasional yellow cur that came out and barked at us as we went by was the only other form of animal life to be seen. From time to time we passed a dwelling, a square cabin of gray unpainted boards, always tightly closed and the dwellers always absent somewhere on business. The only distinct proof I ever saw of the human habitance of these silent, lonely homes was a tiny pair of butternut trousers fluttering on the clothes-line. The minute American citizen who should have occupied these trousers was invisible, and I greatly fear they were perhaps his only pair.

. . . We climbed and climbed; always at tremendous speed, and always the land growing more desolate, and wildly drear, like the cursed site of some prehistoric Sodom, sown with salt. The air shone with a luminous clearness undreamable in coast countries, and at night the stars were huge and fierce: not the soft-gleaming palpitant planets of tropic nights, but keen and scintillant as swords. . . There was something hideous and brutal in the doom laid upon this unhappy territory, as of a Prometheus chained on the mountain-tops; its blood dried to dust in its veins, and lifting a scarred face of gray despair to the rainless sky.

From time to time we crossed a feeble, trickling stream; but no verdure marked the course of its waters bitter and fruitless as tears. During the night our way lay through that still more desolate portion of this dry region named, with simple and expressive literalness, the Bad Lands; and here again I saw a most wonderful coming of the light. The moon, wan with the dawn, hung directly in the zenith, and on the eastern rim of the ghostly gray plain, under the quivering jewel of the morning star, burned the first vague flush of day. Slowly a dusky amethyst radiance filled the sapphire bowl of the sky, quenching the stars one by one as it rose, and when the sun showed over the world's edge the cup was brimmed, and the pale moon shone faintly in its depths, like the drowned pearl of the Egyptian queen. There was no eye but mine to see, yet in the midst of unpeopled desolation the majestic ceremonies of the sky were fulfilled with the same slow pomp and splendor as if all the worshippers of the Sun knelt in awed wonder to see the Bridegroom come forth of his chamber.

. . . Our speed through this part of the country was terrible. Five hours away from Ogden we were two hours and a half behind the time set for our arrival there. Some three quarters of a million hung upon our arriving promptly and getting the track clear for ourselves beyond, not to mention many other important considerations that could scarcely be reckoned in figures; for a great government contract for mails would be either lost or won by morning. A certain engineer, whose name was Foley—or words to that effect—was telegraphed to meet us at the next stop. He was a gentleman of Irish extraction who labored under an entire absence of physical timidity, and who remarked with jovial determination, as he climbed into the cab, that he would "get us to Ogden—or hell, on time." Several times during that five hours' ride the betting stood ten to one on the latter goal, and Hades was hot favorite. The grade at this part of the road has a descent of 93 feet in a mile, and the track corkscrewed through gorges and cañons with but small margin between us and destruction. To these considerations Mr. Foley was cheerfully indifferent, and pulling out the throttle he let the engine have her head at the rate of sixty-five miles an hour. The train rocked like a ship at sea, and sleepers held to their berths in terror, the more nervous actually succumbing to *mal de mer*. The plunge of the engine, that now and again whimpered affrightedly in the darkness, could be felt through the whole train, as one feels beneath one the fierce play of the loins of a runaway horse. From the rear car the tracks were two lines of fire in the night. The telegraph pole reeled backwards from our course and the land fled from under us with horrible nightmare weirdness. The officers of the train became alarmed and ordered speed slackened; but Mr. Foley, consulting his watch, regretted with great firmness that he could not oblige them. One man rolled in an anguish of terror on the floor; and the General Manager, engaged in a late game of whist, regarding the sufferer with sympathetic interest as he took the odd trick with the thirteenth trump, remarked that it was such episodes as this in American life that made us a nation of youthful gray-heads.

We arrived in Ogden on time.

Mr. Foley dismounted with alacrity from his cab, remarked that these night rides were prone to give a man cold, and went in pursuit of an antidote behind a swinging Venetian door on the corner, and we saw him no more.

From here the vast, desolate uplands, 8000 feet high in the keen dry air, showed no further sign of human habitation between the stations, and were ornamented only with the frequent jack rabbit, the occasional coyote, and now and then an arrangement of tepees. Indians crowded about the train at every stop; those of the female sex who were blessed with offspring permitting us to view the living contents of the corded parcels they carried on their backs in exchange for small current coin. The pappoose, I discovered, is the original Baby Bunting. He slumbers with stoical composure in a nest of rabbit skins—presumably those for which "papa went a-hunting"—that line a portable wooden cradle into which he is strapped, and from which, I am told, he rarely emerges during infancy. The girls and boys from six to sixteen I found very pretty, with smooth red skins, glittering teeth and eyes, and black Vandyked locks. Those whom years had overtaken were indescribably wrinkled and parched. Old squaws squatted in the dust huddled in blankets, and were as impassive as ancient worm-eaten idols. A coin dropped into their hands brought a mumble and a glance from their rusted eyes; but indifference did not wound them, neither did the fast train or any of its passengers excite their curiosity—the vagaries of the white man were so numerous that nervous prostration would be a sure consequence of any attempt to interest themselves in his doings, and peace and composure lay only in entirely ignoring him.

All through this country the air had a delicious dry perfume, like the smell of parching vegetation, that was stimulating and wholesome as the resinous incense of pines.

The night before reaching San Francisco we found our first trees again, at a little wayside eating station, where a long row of poplars stood up stiffly in the dusk near our path, and a tiny fountain plashed with an enchanting, cool melodiousness. . . The air was soft and spring-like and the moist darkness pleasant with a smell as of white clover. It could not, of course, in November, have been really the sweet early flowers of the grass, yet I know nothing else that gives out the same clean, delicate perfume; nor can I guess from what that pure vernal fragrance did arise, that was like the first breath from a promised land after long wandering in a country of wilderness and drought.

Sacramento stopped us for a moment at daylight, and here we found rich, juicy verdure, watery marshes, and the first outer edges of that yellow wave from China which has broken upon the Pacific coasts. Still there were no trees. Only grassy, rounded hills, with white sea-mists trailing among them. A country much like that about Newport, but without that icy breath always in the air of the upper Atlantic coast. There was a certain genial tenderness in this atmosphere that even in the hottest day of August the eastern coast never knows.

. . . At fifteen minutes past nine the nose of the ferry-boat from

Oakland touches the San Francisco wharf. We have crossed the continent in four days and twenty hours—thanks to Mr. Foley—and the distance between New York and the Western metropolis is reduced by a whole day. A great achievement! There are crowds of reporters waiting to interview everybody; General Manager, engineer, conductor—even me. We splash cheerfully through the warm rain and oozing mud—the wet season began two days ago—with pleased faces that our tremendous journey is over, walking with free strides and swinging arms because of the long, cramping confinement.

To my eyes, accustomed to the soaring loftiness of New York architecture, this city seems astonishly low. Three or four stories at the most the average is. Because of earthquake they say; but latterly these have almost entirely ceased to occur, as if the land had grown to realize that civilization would not tolerate such impulsive ways, and had gradually abandoned them shamefacedly, as being in extremely bad taste. Consequently a few of the more recent buildings have begun to climb, Babel-like, into the dripping skies.

One gets a remarkable impression of newness here such as a Londoner might on his first landing in New York. Everyone tells you, "I have been here a year—six months—three months—three years." One begins to believe that no one was ever born here. All the buildings look new and fresh, and the whole atmosphere of the place is charged with a vigorous, disrespectful sort of youth.

The city, or at least the Spanish part of it, was founded in the year of the Declaration of Independence, but the American town is only forty or fifty years old. The hotel at which I stop was erected in 1875. It is a huge caravansary, built around a square and enclosing a vast asphalted court adorned with palms and ferns. There is an arcade within this court where the typical American hotel frequenter tips back his chair, reads the papers, and smokes. On the outer side of the arcade are shops of every description, so that one may purchase all the ordinary needs of life without leaving one's lodging-place.

I find here that my progress must be arrested for two days, as the arrangements for hurrying the departure of the ship have fallen through; and I do not altogether grieve, for this tremendous pace for thousands of miles across the country has told upon my nerves to an absurd degree, and I wonder, as I shiver with exhaustion and tremble with nameless, undefined apprehensions, how the coming generation that is to travel a hundred and a hundred and fifty miles an hour will bear the strain of it.

Some process of adaption to a nerve-destroying environment will take place doubtless, humanity being so elastic in such matters.

Meantime there is some space to investigate this first one of the many great cities I must pass through. The editors of the San Francisco "Examiner," who have shown me every courtesy from the moment of my arrival, invite me to luncheon at the Cliff House, which stands on the very western edge of the continent, upon one of the pillars of the Golden Gate.

There is still a soft, warm rain falling when we start. Roses climb around the porches of the residences and hang heavy-drenched blossoms amid their shining wet leaves, perfuming the damp city streets with delicious garden odors. Should I shut my eyes to the hills I mount and descend, the warmth, the humidity, and the rose odors would make me believe myself in New Orleans again. . . In that far distant city I might be going on just such an expedition as this to Spanish Fort on the Lakeside. It gives me a sense of nostalgia, not for the people and city I have but just left, but for an earlier home, where I would have found just such carelessly happy geniality as among these witty, good-looking men who regard the delays of a train with amiable indifference, and see their day slip from them with the carelessness of a spendthrift.

The train crawls along the edge of the harbor shut in between the grassy, treeless hills. We wind around their flanks in perilous fashion for some space, for the harbor juts deeply into the land, and as we cling to their steep sides we hear the waves dashing beneath. There is a sudden turn at last, and before us lies spread the Western Ocean! . . . There is a joyous shock of astonishment in the sight. . . A sense of discovery, of splendid vastness, of a rich new experience seized and dominated. For one keen instant not he who stood

"Silent upon a peak in Darien"

felt a more magnificent dilation of spirit than I.

We lunch, jovially and sumptuously, upon the sea's edge. Already the day is declining as we finish. The rain has ceased, and in the west the curtain of cloud lifts. On a balcony that overhangs the water we watch the sunset. Three great crags stand up sharply two hundred yards away—Seal Rocks—covered with grumbling, barking sea lions, the city's pets, whom the law protects. They look much like fat pigs from this distance. At the last moment the sun flames out gloriously; reddens all the heavens, and gilds a rippling road for me across the waterly world I must traverse. It is a sign of promise, they tell me.

The ride home in the cable car is a curious experience. The streets are of the most astonishing steepness still, though millions have been spend in grading the hills. On each of the cars is a small open space in front where one may sit if one likes and enjoy the sensation of plunging down the most startling inclines and yet see the car stop short at perilous points to allow a traveller to leisurely dismount. The road leads past the famous Nob Hill, where the bonanza kings have their residences— huge wooden palaces of the most rococo designs. It is said that these half-dozen residences cost $9,000,000 to build. James C. Flood's house is of brown stone, the only dwelling of that material in the state, all of the stone having been imported from the East at prodigious expense. One of these palaces—the property of a bonanza relict—is of a curious lead color, which, with its overwhelmingly ornate decorations, gives it an odd resemblance to a gigantic hot-air stove.

There were beautiful public gardens, great public buildings, and many relics of the ancient Spanish domination to be seen in this charming city, but my flight was too rapid to pause for these. That night I saw the quarter known locally as China Town, peeped into some of the huge, splendid theatres and restaurants, and then, at three o'clock the next day, set sail for Japan.

Second Stage

Amid my dreams has always been a carefully elaborated and favorite one of the day upon which I should at last set out on my travels. I had thought out all the details of this episode, and what my emotions should be—a tasteful mingling of regret and exultation—as I bade my unfortunate home-staying friends adieu, and the great Cunarder swung free from the docks, bearing me away to the delights and mysteries of foreign lands. Even in my childhood my sympathy for the heroes in the fairy tales was always keenest at the moment when they waved their hands in farewell and turned their faces at last towards the magical adventures that stalked about impatiently awaiting their advent in the strange countries where their havens lay. So it was a matter of active regret to me that by leaving America from the other side of the continent, this long-dreamed-of incident on the Cunard pier was forever robbed of the salt of novelty.

The White Star steamship Oceanic, of the Occidental and Oriental line—Charles H. Kempson commander—sailed from San Francisco at three o'clock Thursday afternoon of November the 21st, and I found it even under these circumstances a very exciting thing to leave one's country for the first time.

It was much as I had imagined the other picture: the cabin full of ornate flower pieces; luggage thumping down the companion-way; people running back and forth with the apparent purposelessness of ants in a hill; and the friends of the departing standing about in that helpless discomfort and uselessness that make even those whose hearts are torn by the separation long to be gone and put them out of their awkward misery.

Many of the pleasant acquaintances I had made in this short visit to San Francisco had come to bid me God speed, accompanied by a delegation who had got wind of my eccentric performance and came with no other credentials than a desire to gape. This was a figure not in my original picture. The whole army of martyrs to curiosity had afflicted me sorely in those two days on the Pacific coast, sending up their cards in the hotel with urgent messages, and on admission confessing with placid impudence that their sole excuse for this intrusion was a desire to look at me—presumably as a sort of inexpensive freak show. Experience demonstrated, however, the high and delightful effectiveness of an elaborate and astonished civility, that never failed to reduce their robust self-confidence to limp and writhing embarrassment in exactly three minutes, after which discovery I put the heathen to the edge of that manner and smote them hip and thigh. . .

It must be admitted that my emotions on the occasion of this departure were much less tastefully mingled than I had planned they should be, low spirits and loneliness being such active ingredients that they disguised all other flavors, and it is to a little incident I shall forever remember with pleasure that I did not leave America quite unmixedly miserable. At the moment when the gong had warned all visitors ashore there was handed up to me from the wharf a great nosegay of white chrysanthemums and roses, to which was attached a card inscribed "J. M. Prather," and bearing "good wishes" and "New Orleans" pencilled in the corner. A hat was lifted from a handsome gray head, and two kind dark Southern eyes gave me a smile of such friendliness and good-will that it warmed my heart like a greeting from my own people. This unknown gentleman taking the trouble to bid me a silent, fragrant farewell seems to me the most delicate and charming impulse of that much-misinterpreted and scoffed-at Southern chivalry, and should he ever see this I wish him to know how pleasant and lasting was the perfume of his flowers and kindly thought.

Perhaps this is the proper moment to speak of a feature that was to me one of the most interesting of this unusual voyage. I was a young woman, quite alone, and doing a somewhat conspicuous and eccentric thing, yet throughout the entire journey I never met with other than the most exquisite and unfailing courtesy and consideration; and if I had been a princess with a suite of half a hundred people I could have felt no safer or happier. It seems to me this speaks very highly for the civilization existing in all travelled parts of the globe, when a woman's strongest protection is the fact that she is unprotected. I owe a gratitude beyond all adequate expression for the good-will shown me everywhere. It would require many pages to catalogue the names of those who gave up their comfort to insure mine, who considered no trouble of consequence if it secured me from annoyance and disappointment, and who spared no exertion to make my journey speedy and comfortable. In every port I touched I found the kindest of welcomes, and I believe I have put a girdle round the earth of warm and generous friends whom I shall always remember with affection and gratitude. The staff of the San Francisco "Examiner," T. D. McKay, the Burlington Passenger Agent, the owners and officers of the Oceanic, Lieutenant Mitchell McDonald, the Norddeutscher Lloyd people, and my fellow-passengers everywhere are among those who assisted me by every means in their power to effect my object and make my journey agreeable.

. . . The last wooden link with the shore is withdrawn. There is a fluttering storm of handkerchiefs—a brief space of water in the beautiful bay—and then we pass away to the west through the Gates of Gold.

. . . America sinks out of sight, slowly—a vision of green hills in level sunshine. We are divided from it now by a long ridge of whirling foam—the bar, where we begin to rise and fall with the first pulse of the sea. Even that vanishes at last and we plunge forward lonelily on the heaving, dusky plain. The wind of the coming night is cold, and the fluttering paper prayers the Chinese passengers cast overboard to insure a safe voyage it catches and whips sharply away, like autumn leaves falling in the November night.

Not yet have the four hundred pigtails in the steerage composed themselves for the voyage. They run to and fro with queer-colored parcels of strange shapes and keep up a ceaseless, shrill, guinea-fowl chatter, very cheerful in tone. Most of them are going home to settle down upon money made from the "foreign devils," and whatever happens they can laugh.

Even up on the hurricane deck the chill sea wind is tainted with that clinging, pervasive odor that one comes to recognize as "the Chinese smell." No cleanliness can combat it. The ship from stem to stern is wonderfully clean, yet never in the whole voyage is one quite free from the sense of it. Pierre Loti declares it can be smelt on the Chinese coast, while the ship is still miles at sea. On analyzation it appears to be compounded of the bitter fumes of opium and the smoke of incense sticks. An object once permeated by the odor is never rid of it again, and all China reeks of these strange stifling fumes.

I smelt it first in the Chinese Quarter of San Francisco—a place that left a sinister, menacing impression upon my mind. A sense of this being the first gnawing yellow of an overwhelming flood—forced forward by the irresistible propulsion of an over-population behind. One more of those huge, blind migrations of hunger which, like a tidal wave, have obliterated flourishing peoples and races in the full flush of power and civilization, nations who have vanished as herbage vanishes before the gigantic, myriad voracity of desert locusts. Conquered by the mere dead weight of numbers that fill up interposing gulfs with countless dead, bridging all moats between food and that pitiless, relentless famine.

China has 500,000,000 of population, each unit trained by generations of bitter struggle for survival to an industry and economy almost superhuman. California has already nearly 100,000 of them; 30,000 living in San Francisco. Every westward-going steamer carries from three to four hundred home, men who have in a short time secured a competence, and are returning to enjoy it; and yet their number in America apparently suffers no diminution. Fenced out by law from California, the wave flows around this obstacle into British Columbia and trickles back, drop by drop, into the United States. We do not assimilate them as we do our other immigration. They hold to their own national dress, manners, and food. That part of San Francisco abandoned to them grows daily liker a Chinese city. They gut standing houses and reconstruct the interiors to suit their needs. Outside, lanterns hang in front of doors that have Chinese signs, and above these, frail balconies are strung about the windows where jars of chrysanthemums droop their ragged blossoms over the sill. The air is thick with Oriental odors. Street stalls expose for sale vegetables and fruits unknown to us, and the tiny shops with their Chinese furnishings and inscriptions sell wares which no American seeks.

. . . At eleven at night this transplanted city of Cathay is still all alive; the streets crowded with a moving stream of black blouses and yellow faces—everyone cheerful, chattering, and wide awake. The shops stand open, and workmen continue their labors as if it were still high noon. In a basement, a few steps down from the street, gold workers toil in a little black room, seven by ten; a wheezy gas jet flares above their heads, and directly in front of each, on the work bench at which they sit, is a small bowl of cocoanut oil in which smoulder faintly a handful of thin white racines. The flame from these, with a blowpipe, softens and fuses the metals in which they work. Though the place is so narrow and squalid, the bracelets and clasps in process of manufacture—ornamented with ingeniously varied chisel marks— are of considerable value. The workers are impassively indifferent to our curiosity. They work without raising their eyes as we handle their goods, and do not even glance up as we leave, toiling on unhurriedly, though the night is half spent. Here, as everywhere, tiny corkscrews of pungent smoke curl up from a bunch of smouldering Joss sticks stuck in a little earthenware bowl of sand.

. . . Plunging through a narrow door, we grope along a low, tortuous passage, descend to the cellar by rickety, greasy stairs, thread more back corridors, where, in little branching rooms, somnolent bundles lie motionless on shelves—sodden with poppy fumes, past greasy, hot kitchens and cackling cooks, with hissing midnight meals in preparation—and emerge at last into a crowded apartment where men with hideous masks and flaming dresses—like mediæval devils in a mystery play—stand idly about waiting for a cue, and others, radiant and befeathered as tropical birds, pass to the stage by the two doors.

. . . A hideous din of banging, scraping, and clashing of brass. Above all a shrill monotonous chant in a penetrating falsetto. It is the green-room and wings of the *Dom Quai Yuen* —The Elegant Flower-House— where the gems of the classic drama of China are enacted, and where the actors lodge, eat, and smoke their opium.

The performance began at four in the afternoon, and has gone on without intermission ever since. It will end at twelve.

Rapid changes of costume—stiff with gold needlework—are taking place. Faces are being painted—those of the fiends with Oriental ingenuity of hideousness—huge beards are assumed, and gorgeous head-dresses with flags and long pheasant feathers waving above them. We go through the left door and sit on the stage, as if it were the time of Queen Bess and this was one of Mr. William Shakespeare's new plays.

The play goes on, undisturbed by our presence, the actors carefully stepping to one side as they pass us.

The auditorium is packed tight as a sardine box with standing Chinamen who listen as long as they find it amusing and then go away. Up in the gallery two or three sheep-faced Chinese women lend a somewhat indifferent attention.

The heat is frightful. . . There are no windows and but one door, and the smell is overpowering. Not a stench of unwashed bodies, as in a low-class Caucasian crowd, but this same strangling mixture of opium and incense. By contrast even the ill-smelling streets are delightful, and we escape.

The detective, who bears himself with amiable, scornful courage in this resort of "Highbinders," leads the way through fetid, crime-stained alleys. A loud warning note sounds from somewhere near us, and in an instant the street swarms with men passing composedly with their hands under their blouses. The detective turns into a low room with a double nail-studded door. A table covered with a strip of matting and two benches are the only furniture. The owner is calmly smoking a cigarette, apparently engaged in some remote and subtle ratiocinative process. Ten seconds ago, in this room and fifty others, the game of fan-tan was in furious progress. That one note emptied them all.

. . . We mount stairs to a dingy Joss-house, where more incense sticks burn before a trinity of calm-eyed idols—the God of the Sombre Heavens, the God of the Southern Seas, and the God of Happy Wealth—and stroll through the rooms of a restaurant beautiful with carvings and silk hangings, Kakamono and marble and ebony furniture.

. . . But the night wanes and our heads are giddy with this clinging, sickening odor. We will go back to the hotel.

It is the smell of the Chinese sailors and passengers that wakes the memories of the strange sights and sounds.

. . . The night is cold. Top-gallant sails are being set to catch the rising evening wind, and the cries of the pig-tailed yellow seamen are shrill and raucous, like the interjectional and acrimonious talk of cats on a back fence.

It is time to go below and prepare for the first night at sea.

For the next four days my only memory of the Pacific Ocean is of a foaming flood of emerald that roars past my port-hole, making a dull green twilight within. I see only this and the slats of the upper berth. There are six of these slats. Of this I am unwaveringly sure—though I am not usually accurate about figures—because I counted them several thousand times. It was the only mental process of which I was capable during the long nights while I lay and listened to the loud combat of the thundering squadrons outside, whose white plumes flashed into sight again with the first gray gleam of day—the battle still raging. Every plank in the ship creaked and groaned, and shrieked without once pausing to take breath, and I regarded with contemptuous indifference the frantic tobogganing of my most treasured possessions all over the stateroom. What were the fleeting things of this world to one to whose unexampled sufferings death must soon put a period? It was comforting to think that one's last will and testament was made, but hateful the contemplation of burial at sea. It was such an unnecessarily tragical end to this ridiculous wild-goose chase.

The fifth day the boiling pot of the sea subsided, and I began to take beef tea and resolution to live. Other women were also beginning to straggle back to life on deck—pale, wan, and with neglected hair tied up in lace scarfs. They lay in steamer-chairs swathed in rugs, and were indifferent about their appearance and to the charms of conversation. The week was nearly done before the whole ship's company assembled at table, and we began to take note of our fellow-voyagers in this water caravansary.

It was a cosmopolitan crew—Norwegians, Russians, English, French, Japanese, Americans, Germans, Hungarians, and even one Manx-man—our chief-engineer, with a pleasant "out-country" flavor to his speech, and full of tales of a profoundly esoteric humor—a kindly, mellow nature, like one of William Black's old Highland lairds.

There is the Englishman who has made his fortune in China and retired, and is bringing a new-made wife out, by way of America, to see the East, where he had lived so long—an angular English girl, containing the potential British matron, who knits gray stockings and keeps herself carefully aloof from acquaintances that might be detrimental in the future.

The typical American girl is with us, travelling alone—greyhound-waisted, tiny of foot, clad with tailor-made neatness, and armed with an amateur photographer's outfit. She is on her way to visit the American Minister to Japan.

And a couple from Georgia, who have lived twenty years in Los Angeles, but have lost nothing of their genial old-fashioned Georgia ways and looks, and still speak with a soft Southern drawl.

We have a full cargo of missionaries—fifteen in all—mostly young women, and, on this occasion, all Presbyterians. There is much missionary travel back and forth on this line, for the work of proselytization in China and Japan goes briskly on. Among them is a young doctor, who has just taken her degree, and is going to the East to save both souls and bodies. She wears "reform" clothes, and has a strong, well-cut face, from which the heavy hair is brushed smoothly back. She regards the ten years' exile into which she is entering as merely the apprenticeship of her professional career, and is likely to consider the physical welfare of her patients of more importance than the acceptance of her creed. She is the plain, wholesome product of Northwestern life and a Northwestern female college—speaking the speech of that region with a broad and blurring R. . . Her future is simple and pleasant to guess at.

One is less sure of the handsome, slim girl of twenty with deep-set gray eyes, and the delicate pointed fingers of what the palmists call "the psychic hand," indicating undue spiritual intensity of nature. In a spasm of the romantic exaltation to which young women of her age are subject, she has condemned herself to a decade of lonely exile in a remote Japanese town; but a pair of enchanting dimples in her fresh young cheeks war with the maiden severity of her earnest eyes, and she is not indifferent to a young girl's natural joys, though she mentions them loftily as things in the remote past appealing to her—now forever put away. It would be pretty and amusing, as a girl's *exalté* fancies are sometimes, were not the sacrifice of her best young years to indifferent heathen not so real and so melancholy to think on. One is tempted to pray that some Cymon may come to rescue this Christian Iphigenia from her squalid little Oriental altar before the knife of distaste and ennui shall have murdered her youth and charm.

. . . The sea is becoming very blue.

The emerald fades as we pass into these vast liquid fields, and the blue deepens and deepens until one finds no words to express, no simile to convey, the intensity of its burning azure. Sapphires would be pale and cold beside this sea—palpitating with wave shadows deep as violets, yet not purple, and with no touch of any color to mar its perfect hue. It *flames* with unspeakable, many-faceted splendor, under a sky that is wan by contrast with its profundity of tint, and the very foam that curls away from our wake is blue as the blue shadows in snow. The cutter-like prow of our ship flings up two delicate plumes of pearl, and the sunlight shining through these has wrought upon the blue floor beneath us a rainbow arch that encircles our onward path, moves with our moving, and shimmers upon the waving flood as the iris shimmers upon a peacock's breast. . .

It is here enormously deep. The longest plummet line ever let into the sea went down here, and only found bottom at the depth of 4000 fathoms. If one should choose this place to be cured of the wound of living he could never reach the firm earth beneath. He would hang forever in these soundless, icy depths, moving scarcely at all with the slow, obscure flux of the deep-sea tides, surrounded by strange, formless, protoplasmic life, blind, senseless, and inert—the germs from which through billions of years he himself had risen—working out here in these blue solitudes of silence the mysteries of generation and upward growth. He would never perish or be devoured or reabsorbed like his fellows, but age after age would lie enclosed as in a frozen blue gem, with burial more splendid and secure than the Pharaohs. . . The voyage is a lonely one. In all these many thousand miles we never see a sail or any shore. There is no sea life about us, save of the sword-winged birds that follow us from San Francisco to Japan without sign of fatigue, wheeling easily after us as we plunge onward at the rate of three hundred and fifty miles a day, and having quite the appearance of loafing along and waiting for us to catch up. It fills one with a sort of despair to get up every morning and see the same sea, the same horizon, the same birds—nothing to mark our progress except the figures marked each day at noon on the map hanging over the companion-way.

Our small, circumscribed world daily grows in importance in our estimation. We know intimately the characters, tastes, and histories of our companions. We take each other's photographs, and exchange warm professions of friendship; we advise each other about the future, and confide the incidents of the past. We play draughts and quoits and cards; we get together in corners and criticise the missionaries and are criticised by them—and all the while go steadily westward and westward, driven by wind and steam. . . With all our brown sails spread, we fleet through the moonlight with stately courtesyings. Calm mornings dawn behind us. We sail under the vast arches of rainbows that rise out of the water but half a mile away from the ship and span the whole heavens; and at evening the sun falls into the sea, straight before us, amid unimaginable flames and glories, where for an hour we rise and fall on the heaving bosom of the ocean in a great dream-world of jewelled splendor of sapphire and gold, of purple and pearl. . .

This lonely vessel swarms with life. Down in the steerage are over four hundred yellow people. . . All sorts and conditions of Chinamen going home with their earnings. Many are merchants who have a merchant's pass, which enables them to return to America when their business across the water is finished. One old gentleman with an iron-gray pigtail is a "Forty-niner." He came to California during the gold fever, and is now going home to die in China, having thriftily calculated that it costs less to cross the waters alive than it does in a coffin. He was rich in those early days, but, as he explains in fluent and profane American, fan-tan, poker, euchre, and horse races have reduced his store to an immodest competence. However, as he nears the Chinese shore he feels he can afford to wear a magnificent and lurid pair of brocaded trousers, of the sort popular in China when he left, and still—after forty years—of the very latest fashion.

Down in these Chinese quarters, placed where he can catch the best of the healing salt breezes, is a young fellow of six-and-twenty, who lies motionless all day, with crossed hands and half-closed eyes. These hands and the sunken face are the color of old wax, as impassive as if indeed they were cut from some such substance.

It is common among the emigrants to America to fall sick with a consumption and to struggle back in this way to die at home. He seems afraid to breath or move, lest he should waste the failing oil or snuff out the dying flame ere he reaches his yearned-for home—the Flowery Kingdom—the Celestial Empire!

On the after-deck fan-tan rages all day long; also an intricate game of chess, or dominoes, when a less dangerous amusement is desired. Forward there is a space for women, where five or six *retroussé*-eyed females find a temporary home. They are gentle, mild-faced little creatures, who are quick to give smile for smile and answer English amiabilities with what appears to be equally amiable Chinese. All the sailors are Chinamen, and are popular with the commanders. They are obedient, not given to strikes at inconvenient moments, and are under the control of a boatswain, one of their countrymen with a keen, shrewd face and an air of unquestioned authority. He hires them and pays them their wages, and the owners reckon with him alone. He is a person of consequence and wealth, and owns much real estate in San Francisco, sufficient proof that the Chinese, as the white Jack Tar, is the victim of fraud and oppression.

These ships, like those of the merchant Antonio, voyage to the East for cargoes of tea, silk, and spices. There are three lines between China and America; two, the Pacific Mail and the Oriental and Occidental—controlled by the Central Pacific Railway magnates, Huntington, Crocker, and Stanford—have their termini in the United States, and the Canadian Mail sails from Vancouver. They carry out to China returning subjects of the yellow emperor, passengers for the East, flour, Connecticut clocks, hats, shoes, and such select assortments of Yankee notions as are required by the Barbarian.

Returning, they fetch hundreds of bales of raw silk, worth $700 apiece, which must be rushed across the continent immediately upon arrival, and have left the ship and are on their way across the country to the Eastern mills before the passengers have landed. The usual cargo is from 1200 to 1300 bales, and in June the tea trade begins, 1700 to 2700 tons in every ship—the whole of the Formosa crop, some 6,000,000 tons, comes to us. The English will not drink the light, perfumed Oolong. They demand something coarser and stronger. Spices, pepper, and tapioca come from Singapore, and gambier in great quantities for coloring American beer, with thousands of bales of gunnysacks from Calcutta for American wheat, and, from Manila, hemp and jute.

At last there comes a day when one rises in the morning and the sailors, pointing to the horizon, say, "That is Japan," and one cries with cheerful excitement, "Yes! yes!" though there is nothing but the same monotonous sea and sky visible to the unpractised eye.

The missionaries all land here, and are full of emotion at arriving at the scene of their labors to save immortal souls. The Chinese steerage clatter more noisily than ever, pleased to behold this outlying portal of their home. The Japanese poet Kachi, returning from travels in America, where he has been arranging for translations of his works into English, lifts his head again. He is a grave, mysterious-eyed person, who has not spoken to anyone during the voyage, and has usually had his face—his dark, smooth, mask-like face—hidden behind a French novel.

This face is lit now with a fine patriotic glow as a delicate gray cloud grows up along the edge of the water and slowly a vast cone-like cumulus, a lofty rosy cloud, takes shape and form, gathers clearness of outline, deepens its hue of pink and pearl, melts softly into the gray beneath, soars sharply into the blue above, and reveals—Fujiyama. . . the divine mountain!

Having seen it, one no longer marvels that it dominates the Japanese imagination; that every fan, screen, and jar, every piece of lacquer and porcelain, bears somewhere its majestic, its exquisite outline. Twelve thousand three hundred and sixty-five feet high, it rises up alone and unmarred by surrounding peaks; alone in fair calm beauty—the highest mountain in all the islands. In the old Aino tongue—the Ainos whom the warlike Japanese conquered and drove northward—"Fuji" signified "Mother of Fire," and the Japanese added the word "yama," their general term for all mountains. For more than two hundred years the Mother of Fire has been clad in snows and has made no sign. Traces of terrible ancient rages lie along her ravaged sides; but her passions are all stilled, peace and purity crown her; and he who hath seen Fuji-yama's fair head lifted out of the blue sea and flushed with the dream of the coming day layeth his hand upon his mouth and is silent, but the memory of it passeth not away while he lives.

Third Stage

And it came to pass that on the morning of the 8th day of December we rose up and perceived that we had come unto Fanland. . . to the Islands of Porcelain. . . to Shikishima—the Country of Chrysanthemums. The place across whose sky the storks always fly by day, and the ravens by night—where cherry-branches with pink-and-white blossoms grow out of nothing at all to decorate the foreground, and where ladies wear their eyes looped up in the corners, and gowns in which it is so impossible that any two-legged female should walk that they pass their lives smiling and motionless upon screen and jars. . .

Sailing so long due west, we had at last reached the East. The real East, not east of anywhere, but the East. . . the birthplace of Man, and of his Religions. . . of Poetry and Porcelains, of Tradition, and of Architecture. And I who had come to it from the country of common-sense, of steam-ploughs and newspaper enterprise, bowed my head reverently in the portal of this great Temple of the World, and fell upon my knees, awed by its mysterious age and vastness. . . My heart within me was stirred, and I was led to great recklessness in the use of capital letters.

There lies here, by the gates of the East, a land, as we discovered, stranger and more wonderful even than we had dreamed. Captain Kempson had steered us in sixteen days from the coast of America to where a mountain of pink pearl rose out of the sea; and when the gray clouds about its base resolved themselves into land, we found they were the green hills of fairyland! . . . It is revealed to those who live long enough and who go up and down the earth, and to and fro upon the face of it, that man has never conceived an ideal that is not somewhere a reality. There are women living as beautiful as any of the marble Venuses; there are even men as pure and high-minded as Galahad; there are Edens in existence—perchance, somewhere, there is something nearly resembling Paradise—and certainly the enchanting fairy dreams of our childhood, ravished from us by the cruel misrepresentation of our elders, have an actual existence, yet more fantastic and delicious than our baby minds could ever have imagined, in these islands lying hard by the coast of China. . . Let no one scoffingly set this down as a figure of speech. All who have every set foot on these shores bear the same testimony to the elfin witchery of Nippon—the land of the rising sun. There may be something suggestive, in this name, of that eternal tie between youth and the dawn, because certainly here the people are still children, and possess all a child's sweetness, simplicity, and imaginativeness. . . I spent, alas! less than two days in these fairy islands; but all ballad literature declares with great positiveness (see Thomas the Rhymer, the ballad of May-Janet, Mary of Caldon-Low, and other notorious examples) that, having spent even the briefest moment in the Land of the Fays engenders an unquenchable yearning that must some day, some hour, bring one back again—and with this I comfort my heart. . .

We double a headland, pass a slim white pharos, and we make our way up the long bay to Yokohama. The town has been in existence only since 1859, when Japan opened a few ports to foreign trade, but already it is a place of size and importance; for what the Japanese did, they did thoroughly. They jettied the harbor, built ample wharves and go-downs, and bade their own people confine themselves to the inner town across the canal, and not encroach upon the Europeans.

The queerest craft come to meet us in the bay—light-winged junks with gray and russet sails, so carelessly and crazily built that were the sea to but give them a playful slap she would crush them in an instant to kindling-wood. Their feebleness insures her gentleness, it would seem, for they spread their great butterfly wings and skim along without fear, going far afield for the fishing. Many large ships lie at anchor in the harbor—American men-of-war, English, French, and German merchant vessels, and a few neat Japanese coasters. I am told the Japanese were childishly impatient of the foreign tutelage necessary to acquire knowledge of steam navigation, and in haste to try the experiment of running a boat themselves. Starting off with a native crew for the first time, all went well until it was necessary to stop, and this they suddenly discovered they had forgotten how to do. Great was the panic, and she was driving fast on shore, when one bethought him to put the helm hard down; and then they steamed round and round in a circle for hours until steam was exhausted, and the boat stopped of her own volition. . . After which they went to school again for a bit and learned steam navigation in all its branches.

A cloud of sampans descend upon us as we anchor—craft as crazy as the junks—made of three unpainted boards lightly fastened together, with a sharp prow and wide, high stern, across which the standing boatman lays a long oar, and waggles it carelessly in the water, attaining thereby an astonishing speed. Like a certain famous epitaph, it is "simple but sufficient."

. . . These boatmen are the vanguard of elves from Elfland—small, lithe creatures with good-looking yellow countenances, bearing no resemblance to the flat-faced Chinese, and with thick, shining black locks, through which is twisted a blue fillet. Their dress is of dark blue cotton; sometimes the gown-shape called a kimono, and worn by both sexes; but for the most part a costume much like that worn in England in the time of Henry II—cloth hose to the waist, a short jerkin, and loose sleeveless coat reaching to the hips. These blue coats have on the back a great white circle surrounding decorative Japanese characters which set forth the owner's occupation, so that he who runs may read. The intention is business-like, but utilitarianism in Japan is inseparable from the picturesque, and these portable advertisements only add a new charm to the wearer's delightful queerness. There are boys of ten or twelve in some of the boats with the men—quaint little brats with varying patterns shaved on the tops of their heads, entering into the contest to secure part of the carrying trade with the stern and enthusiastic vigor known only to the small boy of all countries.

I attach myself for the time being to a party of agreeable Americans. One of them, a pretty brown-eyed girl named Madge, finds everything as dear and astonishing a delight as do I; but the Lady—the Other Lady—and the Lay-Brother have been here before, and, knowing the greater joys still in store for us, are impatient and superior. The Gentleman from Germany—always pleased in the pleasure of others—is indulgently sympathetic. We—Madge and I—secretly desire to be ferried over to the pier by one of these elfish ferrymen; but the others are so lofty that we meekly submit to allow a commonplace steam-launch to set us on shore, making the journey with the missionaries, who have much exaltation and baggage.

. . . I move in a joyous dream. Can this be I? . . . I, to whom Japan had seemed as fair and vague as heaven—a place to which only the excessively virtuous and fortunate ever went? . . . And, lo! I, in all the fulness of earthly imperfection, am permitted to see it! . . .

More mediæval folk in blue stand about on the stone pier and welcome us with friendly smiles, and we charter their jinrikishas to take us to the hotel. Now, the jinrikisha is exactly the vehicle in which one would expect to ride in this land of fairy children—large perambulators that hold one person comfortably; but instead of being trundled from behind by a white-capped nursemaid, one of the Henry II gentlemen, who wears also straw sandals and an enormous blue mushroom hat on his head, ensconces himself between the little shafts in front and prances noiselessly away with it. He has legs as light and muscular as a thoroughbred horse, and can spin along with the 'rikisha at the rate of five miles an hour. He can, with few intervals for rest, keep this up all day; he will charge you seventy-five cents for the whole; he will not be winded at all, and will be in a gay and charming temper when the day is done. . .

Our way lies along the Bund, a broad, handsome street on the water-front, with a fringe of slim pine-trees strange of outline as are those one is familiar with upon fans. Other jinrikishas are scampering about. Tonsured doll-babies in flowered gowns, such as one buys at home in the Oriental shops, are walking about here alive, and flying queer-shaped kites, with a sort of calm unconscious elfishness befitting dwellers in fairyland. Two little Japanese ladies with pink cheeks, and black hair clasped with jade pins, toddle by on wooden pattens that clack pleasantly on the pavement. Their kimonos are of gay crape, and their sashes tied behind like bright-tinted wings. Everyone—even the funny little gendarme who stands outside of his sentry-box like a toy soldier—gives us back smile for smile.

The Grand Hotel is at the upper end of the Bund, and here another specimen of the *Moyen-âge* in his stocking feet shows us into beautiful rooms facing the water—rooms with steam-heat and electric bells! . . . The darkness closes down swiftly, but charming things are still to be seen from our veranda. The air is crisp and keen; gay cries and clinking pattens tinkle in melodious confusion from the street below. The 'rikishas have swinging from their shafts now crimped pink and white paper-lanterns, and flit by in the dark like fire-flies. A broad yellow moon rises up from the other side of the water and turns the bay to wrinkled gold, against which the ships and junks show delicately black, as if drawn with a pen; and a few clear black lines of cloud are etched across the moon's path. . .

After dinner we are lucky enough to fall into the hands of Lieutenant McDonald. He is a paymaster in the American Navy, and has been here two years. He knows the place well, and offers to be our guide tonight through the native town. In the flowery hotel-court we find our 'rikishas standing in a row in the moonlight, each with one of the pretty lanterns swinging; and we too flit away behind our sandalled steeds.

Only the whir of our wheels and our calls and laughter sound through the city's quiet, moon-washed ways. Here in the European town the houses of two stories of stone stand flush with the narrow asphalt-paved street. A tiny foot-path runs under the shadow of their tiled caves; but as these are paved with little cobblestones, and the roadway is smooth and clean as a table, no one by any chance ever walks in the foot-paths. Occasionally we meet a figure enveloped in dark, shapeless drapery, or a grave, bland Chinese merchant goes by on his soundless cork soles, but this is the business quarter, and people have gone to their homes on the Bund, or upon the Bluff, where consuls and foreigners of importance reside.

We skim around corners with a shrill ki-yi! of warning; debouch into a great square upon which churches and public buildings face; cross a broad canal where acres of sampans are huddled for the night, and find on the other side Shichiu, the native town. Hancho-dori lies before us, the wide main thoroughfare from which spring hundreds of narrow branches, all swarming with a frolicsome, chattering crowd tinkling about in pattens, their multitudinous tapping making a vibrant musical undertone to the sound of the many voices. . .

The houses, delicate little match-boxes of thin, unpainted wood, fifteen or twenty feet high, and divided into two stories, crowd close together, and give upon the street. The fronts of these houses—indeed, the greater part of the walls all around, are sashes of many tiny panes glazed with white, semi-transparent paper, through which the inner light shines as from a lantern; and the shop fronts are mere curtains of bamboo, rolled up during business hours, and let down when the shop is closed for the night.

. . . Business is not nearly over yet. The Japanese are as little inclined to early bed as the Chinese, it seems, and the tide of trade runs strong. . . From all the eaves swing soft bubbles of tinted light—lanterns of many shapes and sizes. The shops are lit and busy, and contain every need, from crabs to curios, that Japanese flesh is heir to. Here and there cluster flocks of light, portable booths, each also with a swaying lantern, where steaming tea is sold in thimble-cups; where saki may be drunk hot and hot, poured from long-necked porcelain bottles, or trays of queer, toothsome-looking sweetmeats are to be had for coins of infinitesimal value. Along the street lie heaps of fresh vegetables—making pretty bouquets of color, all clean and ready for the pot—or fruits of many sorts massed with skill and beauty; . . . little red oranges in bamboo nets, set about with their own green leaves; plums, pomaloes, and fruits whose names we do not know. Everything, everywhere, is radiantly clean, dainty, and inviting. All the folks, too, are gay and voluble. The children play about unchidden; and one might imagine it, if not corrected, some Festival of Lanterns, the place is so joyous, bright-tinted, and fantastic under the smiling, benignant moon. . .

We are on our way to the theatre—one of the humbler sort, where acrobats do their feats for a few cents, where stage and auditorium are on a level, and both merely platforms. A little gallery to one side is reserved for the moon-eyed babies with whimsically shaved heads; but they come down occasionally and rollic about as they wish, quite unreproved. They are never harsh with children in this fair country, and in return the children display a courteous tolerance of the foibles of their elders that is extremely soothing. A group of tumblers on the stage are going through some supple contortions to the sound of a shrill little pipe and a blattering wooden drum, playing out of time with one another. The whole front of the theatre, a curtain of matting, is rolled up at intervals and, when the feat in progress is at its most thrilling climax, is let fall. This artful proceeding stimulates the interest of the passers-by to such poignancy that they succumb in platoons to the pangs of curiosity, and so crowd the little platform that we depart hastily. . .

More moon and lanterns, more laughter and flutter, more clacking of sandals, and then a Japanese Madame Tussaud's, with pleasing little horrors in wax at the entrance as earnest of more of the same cheerful entertainment within. Here is better music, that, during a naïve pantomime of Japanese ghosts, plays what negroes call a "lonesome tune," in a soft minor key. This does not hold us long, for farther up the street is a large and fashionable playhouse, where we may see the best talent of Nippon. At the box-office are piles of flat sticks, six inches long and two wide, painted with numbers in the native character, which, inquiry reveals, are shoe checks for the many sandals hanging on rows of pegs by the door; for here, as in every other house in Japan, one enters in stocking-feet. In consideration of our being benighted foreigners, we are allowed to retain our shoes. . .

The interior is large and lofty. The common folk occupy the level floor of the pit, marked into squares, where family parties sit on small wadded rugs, and are quite at home, bringing their little charcoal braziers to warm their fingers, furnish lights for their tiny pipes, and keep the teapot steaming. The galleries on two sides are divided into matting-lined boxes, one of which they furnish with chairs, seeing that we display small skill in sitting on our heels. We enter during an entr'acte; and before the stage, which is not deep, but lofty, sways lightly in the draught a gay crape curtain. The men in the pit are smoking or curled up in their rugs snatching a nap, while the women drink tea and gossip, and the children romp all over the house. High up on either side of the stage comes from a latticed box the sound of the samsien and other stringed instruments that make a soft, plaintive, and pleasing music. The play has been going on for three weeks and is to end tonight. A gong sounds, the children are recalled, the men wake, and the curtain being pulled aside shows the front of a Japanese house. Two maids appear from a side door and wait respectfully on their hands and knees for the entrance of their mistress, a man very skilfully painted and gorgeously arrayed, but somewhat too masculine to satisfactorily represent the babyish roundness of the real thing. This lady has affairs of great pith and moment to convey to the maids, who make timidly respectful suggestions, which evidently carry small comfort, for the lady retires depressedly. Her lord, followed by his attendants, next appears— an extremely well-bred and aristocratic-looking person in the daimio dress with the two swords; and one judges by his manner that he can add nothing to the cheerfulness of the situation. While matters are at this stage of melancholy, a great clash of music startles the audience, the curtain is drawn aside from a little room on the opposite side of the house, and a magnificent personage appears, who paces with an awe-inspiring strut along the little raised pathway that leads from this room to the stage. The daimio hastens with his attendants to meet him. It is the great shogun himself, stern of mien, and with fierce, orgulous brows; a very impressive figure, notwithstanding he wears black velvet trousers a yard and a half too long for him, and is accompanied by a train-bearer who skips about and disposes this superfluous length in graceful folds whenever his master comes to a standstill. . . He is the embodiment of the sterner side of the Japanese character—the aristocratic spirit that kept alive a proud feudalism long after Europe had forgotten it; the haughty courage that bid a gentleman expiate his offences only by his own hand; the spirit that has allowed no conqueror to ever set foot on Japanese soil, and still makes these people the bravest and freest race in Asia. . .

This tremendous personage makes short work of the handsome daimio, and stalks away after pronouncing some decree to which the noble bows his head in calm acquiescence. . . Madame and the maids are still more unhappy. . . The shogun appears to have suggested the advisability of the "happy despatch," and the lady fails to appreciate this little attention on the part of her sovereign. An aged and garrulous mendicant next enters, and one guesses at once that this is the element of comedy which is to relieve the gloom of the situation, and probably the humble *deus ex machinâ* who will arrest the tragedy. His acting is extremely clever, and for myself I should like to see how it all turns out; but the smile of the Gentleman from Germany is growing wan, and the Lay-brother, who has no chair, is becoming distinctly cross, and so we go home.

The shops are shut by this time, and we see some curious little domestic episodes shadowed on the paper window-sashes, when householders thoughtlessly pass between them and the lamp. The European town is flooded with a high tide of moonlight, and we are, it seems, the only ones who wake sweeping in a long, swift line through the streets in our silent fairy carriages with the rosy lantern swinging. . .

A nipping and an eager air blows among the rose-trees in the court next morning when Madge and I start out for early shopping. Lieutenant McDonald, magnificent in brown cords and laced Russia-leather riding-boots, offers us his pony carriage, but we scoff at anything less foreign than a jinrikisha, and set off together for Benton-dori, the fashionable shopping-street of Shichiu. In spite of the fall in the thermometer, the spirits of the public in general appear in no way chilled. The bare feet in straw sandals look red and uncomfortable, but the owners of them merely acquire great plumpness of appearance by adding three or four more cotton-wadded kimonos to their costume, tuck their chilly fingers away in their ample sleeves, and laugh at the passing discomfort. Everything looks ridiculously tiny by day, and deliciously absurd. One has a feeling that it is all a game that one is playing to amuse the children. We sit on the edge of the little platform that forms the floor of the shop, and, in the baby talk that is called pigeon-English, bargain with the amiable shopkeeper seated on his own heels and within easy reach of all his goods. Just so one used to play "keep store" in the nursery when one sold one's toys for astonishing sums to wealthy playmates whose purses were bursting with scraps of torn envelopes—fiat money of arbitrary value. We have been instructed not to pay more than half that is asked, but the prices are so delightfully low that we give them joyfully, and without haggling. We wander from shop to shop, received with an air of affectionate friendliness everywhere; we warm our fingers at many different braziers, and might drink little thimble-cups of tea at every hospitable place of business were we so minded. The really valuable bric-à-brac is costly here as elsewhere; but many charming things in common use among the people, pretty proofs of their universal love of beauty, are to be picked up for a mere trifle.

In the silk-shops we find the very poetry of fabrics: . . . crapes like milky opals, with the pale iris hues of rainbows; crapes with the faint purple and rose of clear sunset skies, embroidered with wheeling flights of white storks. Out of a sweet-smelling box comes a mass of shining stuff that the low-voiced fourteenth-century-looking shopkeeper calls by three musical syllables, which, translated, signify the Garments of the Dawn. Its threads shimmer like the crystals of dry snow, and amid its folds the whiteness blushes to rose, deepens to gold, or pales to blue, while through it here and there runs a sort of impalpable cloudiness like a morning mist. He shows us Moon-cloths, duskily azure with silver gleams; . . . crapes, pearl-white and rich with needlework in patterns of delicate bamboo fronds or loose-petalled chrysanthemum-blossoms, . . . fairy garments all, woven of rainbows and moonbeams!

. . . We are in the train going to Tokio. We have lingered too long in the enchanted wardrobes, Madge and I, and are in disgrace with the others for our tardiness, which has nearly lost them the train, . . . but the world is too much to our liking today for even this to depress us, and we feel that the Gentleman from Germany is secretly on our side. It is a funny train, as absurdly toy-like and doll-housey as is everything else in this country; and our destinies are committed today into the hands of a sweet-mannered gentleman in a gray kimono and an American hat, who is to guide us amid the beauties of his country's capital. . . Delicious little pictures run past our car windows, astonishing us with the sudden revelation of what nonsense the Occident has talked about the conventionality of Japanese art, when, in truth, it is the most exquisite fidelity to the nature the artist has seen about him. The world the Japanese artist has painted has been the world just as it exists in his own country, and, moreover, he has in his art caught and expressed with perfect and subtle veracity its atmosphere of gay grotesquerie—of delicate fantasticality—its crisp and fragile fairy likeness—the soul of things about him that has so far escaped the brush of every foreign artist endeavoring to portray the outward forms of things Japanese. . .

The charm of all we see from our car—the Tokaido (the great imperial highway that intersects the whole empire), the queer little farm-houses and railway stations, and even the water-soaked paddy-fields, reaped of their rice—lies in the exquisite, faultless cleanliness and propriety of it all. Nothing is out of place; nothing requires allowance and forgiveness; . . . all is beautifully posed and arranged as if sitting to have itself instantaneously photographed; and the Other Lady, recognizing this attitude of expectancy, the click of her camera is heard in the land. . .

Arrived at Tokio, we go to the residence of the American minister, who is very agreeably housed, and where we find—as in all private dwellings throughout the East—a most astonishing profusion of flowery plants blooming and bourgeoning in every corner of the mansion. We tell the American girl with the camera and the small feet goodbye, for she is remaining here as a guest, and we see the minister's carriage drive up, accompanied with two out-runners in gorgeous native liveries of orange and blue. These out-runners accompany all folk of importance in Japan, and keep pace with the horses without fatigue. A fine, picturesque bit of mediæval swagger they make. . .

We take our tiffin in a little latticed glove-box of a tea-house, the polished daintiness of whose interior will not permit of our wearing our shoes; and a grotesque spectacle they make—those American shoes, standing in a row just inside the entrance while we tiptoe awkwardly and shamefacedly in our stocking-feet up the stairs. A mild diffused light through the paper panes illuminates our tiny upper chamber, whose only furnishings are sweet-smelling mattings, a kakamono hanging on the wall, and a tall jar full of red-berried branches in the corner. We are served by a moon-faced little maid in a flowered gown, who bows at each entry and draws in her breath to signify what a privilege it is to breathe the same air with us, . . . one of the customs of a national courtesy so thorough and far-reaching that even the domestic animals are civilly addressed as Mr. Cat and Mr. Dog. . . She brings us braziers to warm our fingers and wadded rugs to sit upon, tailorwise, and serves us delicious tea, sugarless and straw-colored, in tiny cups without handles, and bowls of rice across which are laid crisp, freshly broiled eels—a delightful dish that we eat with polished black chopsticks.

. . . The 'rikishas race away with us quite to the other side of town—past great forts and fosses, past the mikado's palaces and gardens, to the famous temples at Shiba. The road is smooth and broad and overshadowed by pines. A superb gilded and lacquered gateway admits us to the temple grounds, and here the guide goes in search of a shaven-headed priest who will show us his treasures. Immediately before us stands a lovely red temple, rich with gold and carvings and lacquered figures, and with a marble-paved veranda polished as onyx; but we cannot wait to examine it. We go to the left and climb the hill by stone steps strewn with crimson petals of the camellia blossoms. . . At the end of an avenue of tall gray stone lanterns—where lights shine during the great religious festivals—stands the tomb of Ieymitsu, the son of Ieyasu, the great shogun who usurped supreme authority and reduced the mikado to the position of a primate. But the little finger of Ieymitsu was thicker than his father's loins. He consolidated the feudal system, and chivalry under his rule achieved its noblest development; Japanese arms were feared and respected abroad and at home; and under the sun of his kingly favor Japanese art blossomed into its supreme, consummate flower. Today the curios of his period are worth their weight in gold, and all the knightly traditions of the land cluster about his name and reign.

Laying down a life of power, he yearned for an immortality of beauty—to be magnificent and impressive even in death; and, choosing this spot, he spent millions in glorifying his last resting-place. He had a nice taste in tombs, had this splendid old Japanese. The hill is clothed in pines, through which the light winds go softly sighing. The westering sun shines slantingly along the green arcades and makes golden shadows across the path we have come. The mild-moving air has stolen red blossoms from the glossy-leaved camellia-trees and shred them upon the hoary gray lanterns and mossy stairs. . . Never monarch slept among sweeter verdure, space, and calm. . . The tomb has, as have all these shrines and temples, walls of a deep rich red, whose clear color three centuries have not dimmed. . . Above is a broad frieze of gorgeous carving—dragons, birds, lotus, and chrysanthemums tangled in fantastic intricacies, and all lacquered and gilded with such honest pains that Time's teeth cannot gnaw through the color or his breath tarnish the gold. Above the frieze leans the green and gray tiled roof, with its fretted ridges and airy, upturned gables, of a fine lightness and unmatched grace of outline. . . The interior is octagon-sided and mosaic-paved, and up from the centre, where the great shogun lies, curls the cup of a giant stone lotus, whose calyx is the jewelled shrine, springing to the roof which rests on a ring of polished columns, and each of these in turn on a base of lotus leaves. Everywhere, from pavement, shrine, and wall, shines the shogun's golden crest of three lotus leaves meeting at the stems... Space does not avail to tell of the splendors of this tomb, ... the plating of gold and silver bronze; the myriad-tinted lacquers, hard and polished as gems; the untarnished gilding, the inlaying of precious stones, and, most wonderful of all, the grace and gorgeousness of the myriad delicate fantasies wrought out by art to soothe the king's last sleep.

... "Et ego in Arcadia—I too have been in fairyland!" I cry to the lay-brother as we stroll away in the mild sunshine and down the flower-strewn stairway. He had warned me of the exceeding great loveliness of the place, and, having seen it, I am fain to declare that I forgive fate in advance for any future trick, because of this one day of unmarred delight.

We race across the city again in our 'rikishas to the great park of Uyeno, to see the sun go down behind Fujiyama... to look out across the city's vast hive with its million or more of folk whose myriad lights begin to twinkle in the violet dusk... We worship a moment before a gigantic, calm-lidded stone Buddha set on a little hill, amid a thicket of roses.

Then the railroad again, ... a broad, yellow moon shining on the ever-present Fujiyama, ... regretful farewells to the charming Americans and Lieutenant McDonald, and then the visit to fairyland is over... I must pass on in my swift course, and be ready for new sights and friends.

Fourth Stage

H ong Kong! . . . I like the name of my next port. It has a fine clangorous significance, like two slow loud notes of some great brazen-lunged bell. . . Hong—Kong!

We have one more glimpse of Fujiyama the next morning as Japan sinks out of sight. . . During the day the young Chinaman with the pallid waxen hands dies. He has struggled hard to keep the flame burning until he sees his own land, but the crisp breath of the Japanese coast puffs it suddenly out. A canvas screen is hung across one corner of the steerage deck, and the doctor goes back and forth from behind it. . . They will carry him back to his country, though he will not be glad or aware. But the sea knows she is being defrauded of her rights, and wakes and rages. She comes in the nights and beats thunderously with her great fists upon our doors. She leaps to look over our bulwarks for her hidden victim; she roars with wrath and will not be appeased. For two days we steam in the face of the northwest gale she has raised, and for three the ship plunges like a spurred horse. I find that bodily I am proof now against seasickness, but my temper has a violent attack of *mal de mer*. It makes me bitterly cross to go leaping and plunging about the ship, not to be able to keep my seat, and to gradually collect my soup and entrées in my lap; so I retire to bed, wedge myself in tight with pillows, and go steadily through every word the ship's library affords on the subject of Japan. I am refreshed and cheered to find that the writer of each book fails, as signally as I shall fail, to convey any adequate idea of the fairy charms of the Land of Chrysanthemums. . . Shall one then paint a dragonfly with a whitewash brush? . . .

Nevertheless, I gather from these books much confirmatory of my own swiftly gathered impression. The very faults of the Japanese are such as are misdemeanors in adults but quite forgivable in children. They are hopelessly immodest, with the unconscious shamelessness of babies, and they fib imaginatively with an infant's inability to discern the relative value of truth and falsehood. They are brave with the headlong courage of the child who is ignorant of the meaning of danger, and in matters of honor they have youth's reckless passionate exaltation. They are unfailingly sweet-tempered and courteous. Their artistic conscientiousness ascends into the realm of morality. They are frugal and temperate; they detest all ugliness, dirt, and squalor; they are unique; they are delightful—they are Japanese! . . .

On Sunday, the 15th, we reach Hong Kong. The sea turns to a cool profound emerald, and we descry again on the horizon the bamboo wings of the fishing and coasting junks. These sails are somewhat larger and deeper of hue than those of Japan, and still more resemble the fans of giant yellow and russet butterflies.

. . . More treeless mountains rise out of the green waters. They are broken and rugged; of volcanic origin; and where the scant herbage fails their naked sides show tawny as a lion's hide. It is one of the three beautiful harbors of the world, the water winding deeply inland between the hills, and flowing around island mountains ringed with girdles of foam. At one o'clock we are in the broad antechamber of the port, known as the Lyee-Moon, and are signalled from the lofty peak to the inhabitants of the town lying at its foot. At two o'clock we drop anchor in the roadstead amid a great host of shipping of all character and nations—twenty-three days out from San Francisco. The White Star people had instructed Captain Kempson to make all due haste for my sake, and it is one of the swiftest voyages ever known at this season of the year, when the winds are contrary, coming to the west. We were sixteen days to Japan, where we remained thirty-six hours, and five days from Yokohama to Hong Kong.

The island of Hong Kong is a cluster of lofty abrupt hills with scanty vegetation, seized by England in 1842 after a struggle with China. At that time the town was an insignificant fishing village, but the value of the site was great commercially and strategically. It is a convenient and safe harbor for the squadron detailed to watch and menace the Russian navy in the Pacific; and the English have elevated the village into a flourishing city and made it the fourth shipping port of the world. The harbor is navigable for the largest merchant vessels and men-of-war in existence, and is perfectly sheltered and easy of access.

As in Japan, sampans swarm about us as soon as we are made fast to the buoy, but they are far less picturesque than were those. Each sampan wears a bamboo hood in the stern, and here the owner houses his wife and rears his family. A brood of babies is in each one of these little hutches, and while the pigtailed subject of the Celestial Emperor stands and rows in the bow, his helpmeet sculls in the stern with a long oar that serves as a tiller. The Chinese woman of the working class, I find, decided centuries ago the question still in its stormy infancy with us—of the divided skirt. She clothes herself in a pair of wide black trousers, a loose tunic, jade earrings and cork-soled shoes, and is ready for all the emergencies of life. Should they take the form of marriage with a sampan owner, she will but rarely set her foot on shore again, but will, in common with something like 20,000 of the "water population" of Hong Kong, work, sleep, eat, bear her children, rear them, and die in this crazy little boat.

I am very regretful at leaving the Oceanic, where I have received so much kindness; but "hateful is the dark blue ocean" after more than three weeks of it, and delightful the thought of even three precious days on land. I am to stay with personal friends in Hong Kong in order that I may see something of domestic life in the East; and I am taken ashore in their private steam launch. Chairs and bearers are waiting for us on the dock—comfortable fauteuils of bamboo, trimmed with silver and supported by long bamboo poles. This is even more amusing than the 'rikishas. There are four Chinamen for each chair, dressed in my friend's livery—loose trousers and tunic of white cotton bordered with rose color. Their feet are bare and their queues are gathered into Psyche knots, on the back of their heads, like the hair of the shop girls in America.

They lift the poles to their shoulders and start off in a swift swinging trot. We pass across the narrow strip of level land that lies on the water's edge—the business quarter of the city built handsomely and solidly of native stone—and begin to mount the broad steep ways that lead to the residence quarter. These are cool and shadowy with great trees, with the clattering feathered spears of the tall bamboos, with gigantic ferns, and prodigious satiny leaves of tropical lilies. The streets are paved with asphalt and have no sidewalks; here and there they resolve themselves into broad flights of shallow steps up which the bearers carry us with perfect ease. . . The verdure is magnificent; the town is submerged in it, and flowers are everywhere. On every wall stand rows of earthen jars full of greenery and blossom—rows on rows of them in the courtyards—more rows on both ends of every flight of steps, and on all balcony railings. Every nook and corner that will hold a jar is filled with bloom, and the rarest orchids are strewn carelessly about, industriously producing flowers, in delicious provincial ignorance of their own value and of what they might exact in the way of expensive attention.

. . . We meet the most astonishing varieties of the human race. All sorts and conditions of Chinamen—elegant dandies in exquisitely pale-tinted brocades; grave merchants and compradors, richly but soberly clad; neat amahs with the tiny deformed Chinese feet, sitting at the street corners, taking in sewing by the day; street sellers of tea, shrimp, fruit, sweetmeats, and rice; women working side by side with the men, mending the streets, . . . horrible old women, weazened and wrinkled beyond all imagining, all the femininity shrivelled out of them, their only head-covering a bit of black cloth across their seamed and humble foreheads, and the last pathetic spark of the female instinct for adornment displaying itself in the big jade and silver rings in their ears.

. . . From windows shaded by light bamboo blinds look out coarse olive faces—heavy and dull of eye, repulsively sensual. These are Portuguese; descendants of the hardy sailors who explored and ruled these southern seas before the English supplanted them. They have bred in with the natives everywhere and have grown an indolent mongrel race. . . Plump and prosperous-looking gentlemen go by in European dress and with tight-fitting purple satin coal-hods on their heads. Their complexions are dark and their features—dug out of a mat of astonishingly thick beards—are aggravatedly Hebraic in their cast. They are Parsees, and look uncommonly like the lost tribes—exhibiting also, I am told, the same eminent abilities in business probably possessed by those much-sought-for Hebrew truants.

. . . At the corner stands a haughty jewel-eyed prince of immense stature—straight and lithe as a palm—in whose high-featured bronze countenance are unfathomable potentialities of pride and passion. . . He wears a soldier's dress and sword, and a huge scarlet turban of the most intricate convolutions. I cry out with astonishment at the sight of this superb creature.

"Is it an emperor?" I demand, in breathless admiration.

"An emperor! Poof! it's only a Sikh policeman. There are hundreds about the place quite as splendid as he."

. . . When the Arabs who had seen Europeans only in trousers fled before the magnificent onslaught of the kilted Highlanders at Tel-el-Kebir, they exclaimed in amazement:

"If these are the Scotch women, what must the men be!" so, though a bit dashed, I say to myself, "If these are the Sikh policemen, what must their princes be?" and secretly resolve to go some day and discover.

It gives me my first real impression of the power of England, who tames these mountain lions and sets them to do her police duty. It would seem incredible that this rosy commonplace Tommy Atkins who comes swaggering down the street in his scarlet coat can be the weapon that tamed the fine creature in the turban. . . What is it makes this cheerfully vulgar Anglo-Saxon the lord of the Hindoo? . . . Physically he is not the Sikh's superior, and in profound and passionate sentiment, if one may judge by the countenance, the Hindoo is infinitely above the Briton. Nor is the latter greater in courage or dignity, for these Indians made a noble resistance to English encroachment, and after submission were enrolled in the army of the conquerors as their bravest and most loyal native troops. . . What is the secret? . . . Is it more beef and mutton perhaps—or more of submission to orders and power of self-discipline? . . .

Here comes one of the conquerors of India, a kilted Highlander, swinging down the road in his plaided petticoats, with six inches of bare stalwart pink legs showing, and a fine hearty self-confidence in his mien that signifies his utter disbelief in the power of anything human to conquer him.

We leave this olla-podrida of nations behind, and mount into a broad street curved around the flank of the hill. On the upper side of it is the heavy wall of the Portuguese convent, once painted a lovely light blue, and now freaked and stained a thousand charming tints by time and weather. Creepers bearing great yellow flower disks trail across it; trees shadow it, and the convent's massive outlines loom from behind. . . A beautiful work is done inside in teaching Chinese girls the sweet decencies of life and pretty feminine arts. Opposite is my friend's house—two stories of stone surrounded by great verandas. The coolies run down a curving flight of steps and deposit us at the door.

These Hong Kong houses have admirable interiors. A lofty hall divides this one, terminating on a rear veranda, with a wide view of the precipitous white city, buried in verdure, sloping down to the flashing emerald of the bay, that is ringed with tawny hills. The hall is filled with more potted plants, and massive furniture of Indian ebony and marble. To the left is a great drawing-room, fifty feet long and eighteen high, with a dozen windows. Here are more palms and ferns, rich European fittings, and Eastern bric-à-brac. Scattered about are photographs of all the Hohenzollerns, for my friends are Germans. We rest awhile in the cool green gloom of this apartment, and drink tea brought by a tall yellow gentleman in silk trousers, a black satin cap, and a crisp rustling blue gown reaching nearly to his ankles. My bedchamber is another huge shadowy place, with a dressing-room and bath as large as the ordinary drawing-room at home, furnished with old mahogany and silver fittings brought from Germany two generations ago. Its airy, unencumbered spaces remind me of the fine old bedchambers in the plantation houses at home in the South. . . Here I am awakened in the morning by another pigtailed gentleman, who brings me my tea, prepares my bath, and arranges all things ready for my toilet. Female servants in Hong Kong are rare; and after the first surprise is over these clean, grave male-maids seem perfectly efficient and convenable servitors. Our meals are stately functions—adorned, of course, with profuse greenery and flowers—with fine wines and delicate food exquisitely prepared. . . A sumptuous Eastern life that flows on with cool and unhasting repose and gravity. I was never in a German household before, and find here many pretty unfamiliar customs—one of them a nice fashion of repeating upon rising from the table a German phrase which expresses mutual good-will and affection, a sort of grace of friendship after meat. There is a careful sweet civility too in their intercourse with one another, very pleasant to share.

. . . In all our expeditions about the place we are luxuriously carried by our coolies, who apparently put forth no special effort or haste, but with whom a rapid walker with no burden is unable to keep pace. The streets are a panorama of unending interest. 'Rikishas are employed occasionally in the level part of the town, but the general mode of travelling in the steeper streets is by chairs, the distinctive livery of private bearers consisting of the color of the border of their white garments. Stout, haughty, red-faced Englishmen go by in these chairs, and occasionally a covered one is met, with bamboo blinds, in which sits an equally fat and haughty mandarin. Coolies run about at a dog-trot bearing immense burdens swung at the two ends of a pole carried on their naked muscular yellow shoulders. Pretty round-faced children, dressed exactly like their elders, play in the doorways and exchange smiles with the passer-by. There is a general public amiability—without the gay and gracious vivacity of Japan—in all save the lowest class of laborers. These toil terribly and incessantly for infinitesimal sums, and by the most minute economies manage to exist—to continue these labors and privations. They are old in youth, parched, callous, and dully indifferent. Incapable of further disappointment, they exist with the stolid patience of those who expect only stones and serpents, having abandoned all hopes of bread and fish. . .

The town is growing and prosperous. The shops, hotels, clubs, and counting-houses are handsome stone buildings with deep arcade-like verandas surrounded by pointed arches. The banks and public buildings are imposing and massive, and the place is noisy with the sound of mason's tools. The harbor for 200 yards in front of the Praya (the broad water street) is shallow, and preparations are being made to fill it up and give Hong Kong the benefit of this extra width of level land. The same was done some years ago at Kow-Loon, on the opposite side of the harbor, where England owns a strip of the mainland. On this reclaimed land fine wharves lined with godowns (warehouses) have been built, and huge dry-docks and shipyards established where shipbuilding goes industriously on and the largest vessels afloat can put in for repairs. The export trade in cotton, tea, silk, spices, and rice is enormous, and the place develops year by year considerable manufacturing industries.

Though three great lines of trans-Pacific steamers ply between Hong Kong and America, there is only one resident of that nationality in the city besides the consul. The English, Germans, Parsees, and Chinamen conduct its business. The strategic importance of Hong Kong is so great that four or five war ships are always in its harbor or cruise in the neighborhood, and two full regiments are kept in garrison. At the time of my visit one of these regiments was of Highlanders who wear in this hot climate white jackets and helmets with their kilts. They are being put through a rapid and vigorous drill one morning when we pass the parade ground, and the pipes are shrilly skirling—music to stir the heart in which runs the smallest drop of Scotch blood. Not even the Sikh policemen stand first in my affections at this moment, as, to that wild keen sound, the solid ranks of brawny red-haired Caledonians trot by, with their petticoats fluttering about their bare knees and their bayonets set in a glittering hedge. . . Oh, braw sight! . . . Oh, bonny lads! . . . Scotland forever! . . .

The climate of Hong Kong at this season is of Eden. Airs of Paradise wave through the splendid tropical foliage. The sun is pleasantly hot at midday, and the mornings and evenings are dewily cool. Coolies do their work naked to the waist, but ordinary European garments are comfortable. From every point is seen either the light flashing from green waters, or the red and yellow hills outlined against a turquoise sky. My friends are loath that I should lose a single pleasure, and we are out all day long in this adorable weather. One of our paths lies through the green twilight of the Botanical Gardens, filled with such vegetation as I have always regarded with a doubting eye in the picture of the Asiatic half of the geographies. We pass under the tremulous lacey shadows of ferns twenty feet high, through trellises weighted with ponderous vines that blow a myriad perfumed purple trumpets up to the golden noon, and emerge upon sunny spaces where fountains are sprinkling silver rain upon banks of crimson and orange flowers. The flaxen-haired, muslin-clad English children play here, cared for by prim trousered Chinese amahs; and we meet pretty blue-eyed German ladies in their chairs taking this road home.

Another expedition leads to the top of the peak, whose head is 2000 feet above the water and up whose side the town climbs year by year. Our way—at an angle of forty-five degrees—is by a tram dragged up the mountain by means of an endless chain. This peak is the city's summer resort and pleasuring-ground. Handsome bungalows cling to its steep sides—built in the Italian style, of warm cream-white stone. There is ten degrees difference in temperature between the summit and the town, and a summer hotel is in process of construction at the top. . . We can see from here how the water flows between the hills, and how the harbor broadens to bays and narrows to straits between the island mountains. Only at Rio Janeiro and Sydney, they tell me, is there a harbor whose beauty compares to this. The man in charge of the windy signal station comes out and explains to us the various ways in which the town is warned of the coming of vessels, and also introduces us to an extremely low-spirited and discontented-looking lady with battered features who turns her back on us and stares in unwinking disgust out to sea. She was once the gay and gilded figure-head of the Princess Charlotte, wrecked in these waters long since, and plainly resents what she looks upon as her fall in life, and the banal jocosity of those who rescued her—bobbing detachedly about in a sheltered cove—and brought her up here to assist a low signal officer! . . .

Our chairs have come up another way, and we are to be carried down the long winding road that sinks by slow stages to the town. During the first stage we are in full sunlight, passing under the walls of the white palace-like bungalows with smooth-shaven tennis-courts where ruddy-cheeked, spare-loined young Englishmen toss the bass to fair-haired, light-footed English girls. Then the road—the earth here is a thousand beautiful shades of buff and rose—winds about to the east, and we pass into the shadows. A tiny Greek church with a sparsely populated graveyard clings to the declivity above us, and from far below comes the faint cool sound of waters foaming round the foot of the hills.

. . . The sun has set; only the utmost heights are gilded now, and the twilight deepens on our path. We swing around the hills—in and out, and down, down, with smooth, easy motion—to the regular *pad, pad, pad* of the bearers' feet. Here and there in the dusk we discern the scarlet turbans of Sikh warders, standing motionless as bronze statues. Below in the harbor the lights of the town, the ships, and the flitting sampans sparkle through the faint evening mist like multitudinous fireflies. The town climbs the hill to meet us, and we pass into the still heavier gloom of trees. A great pure calm reigns where we sink into this cool flood of darkness; . . . half-naked figures go by noiselessly on unshod feet. . . I know all this; I remember it well. . . Somewhere—once—I passed through just such shadowy ways in the warm nights. . . This silent peace of darkness after long hours of burning light is quite familiar to me. I try to recall where it was—but it was a long, long, time ago and I have forgotten the name of the place and the people who lived there. . . I only remember that I used to pass under the great trees, . . . that some wonderful secret delight waited for me beyond them. Alas! That was very long ago; to night only an excellent dinner attends my coming. . .

> "In Xanadu did Kubla Khan
> A stately pleasure dome decree—"

Kubla Khan did come to tiffin one day—a handsome dark gentleman of forty years or so, with very white teeth and eyes like black velvet. He wore extremely well-fitting London clothes, and in his soft, slow voice he signified that on the morrow he would take us to see the pleasure dome—not yet entirely complete. . . Kubla Khan was his name in Xanadu of course, but in Hong Kong, for the sake of convenience and brevity, he was called Catchik Chater. Also for convenience and brevity he gave it out that he was a British subject, resident in China, born in India, and with a certain mixture of Greek and Armenian blood in his veins; naturally in Xanadu his rank and pedigree were far more complicated. . . It had been his fancy to come to Hong Kong twenty years before, neglecting to bring with him any drafts on his treasury, and in the interim he had collected something like a million pounds it was said. It was he who had made the long water-front at Kow-Loon, rescuing it from the sea, and had covered it with great godowns filled with merchandise of the East, and it was he who was proposing the same feat on the opposite side of the harbor. He had interested himself more or less in the banks, the shipyards and manufactures of various sorts, and he now felt prepared to erect in China a repetition of the Xanadu pleasure dome. He took us first to see his docks and godowns, resounding with the loud clangors of trade, and then through the grassy Kow-Loon plains, by a wide red road shadowed with banana-trees, to this lordly pavilion set on the crest of many flowering terraces—its pale-yellow outlines cut cameo-like against the burning blue of the equatorial sky. To the right is the naked side of a hill all deep-tinted buff warmed with red, and everywhere else a sea of satin-leaved tropical foliage.

The centre of the pavilion is a great banqueting-hall with domed roof thirty feet above the tessellated pavement. The walls are frescoed in the same deep cream color of the exterior, touched here and there with blue and rose and gold. Twenty lofty arched doors give on the veranda, from whence beyond the roses of the terrace one sees the glitter of the green waters of the harbor. At each end of the banqueting-hall opens a drawing-room set with mirrors and lined with divans. Beneath are tiled bath-rooms, needed in this hot climate after using the tennis-courts and bowling-alleys. Here Kubla Khan's guests come—come by twenties and fifties—and feast splendidly on high days and holidays and on hot star-lit tropical nights. It is like the sumptuous fancy of some splendid Roman noble, pro-consul of an Eastern province. The pavilion for the moment is in the hands of workmen, so we may not dine there; but we do dine with the Khan in his town house, eating through many courses, drinking many costly wines, and served by a phalanx of tall Celestials in rustling blue gowns.

Another day we go to the shops and turn over costly examples of Chinese art—coming home through the many-colored ways of the native town;—steep streets that climb laboriously up and down stairs, and so narrow that there is hardly room for our chairs to pass through the multitudes who swarm there. Sixteen hundred residents to the acre they average in this part of the town, buzzing and humming like the unreckonable myriads insects bred from the fecund slime of a marsh. Two thirds of their life is passed out of doors in the streets, and all seem to be patiently and continuously busy. Children are as the flies in number and activity. The place smells violently; smells of opium, of the dried ducks and fish hanging exposed for sale in the sun, of frying pork and sausages, and of the many strange repulsive-looking meals being cooked on hissing braziers in the streets and in doorways. There is no lack of color. The shops are faced with a broad fretwork richly gilded, and the long perpendicular signs are ornamentally lettered with large black characters. Every house is lime-washed some strong tint, and the whole leaves upon the eye the color-impression one gets from Chinese porcelains—of sharp green, gold, crimson, and blue; all vigorous, definite, and mingled with grotesque tastefulness.

My plan had been to sail from Hong Kong on the Norddeutscher-Lloyd ship Preussen, but a Peninsular and Oriental steamer sails three days earlier; I am advised to go in her as far as Ceylon, and I do. So on the morning of the 18th of December I find myself on the deck of the Thames, surrounded by the charming friends and acquaintances of this Hong Kong episode, who have come to give me a final proof of their goodness, and wish me speed on my journey.

This boat is as polyglot as the land I have just left, and swarms with queer people. The sailors are Lascars, clad in close trousers and tunic of blue cotton check and red turbans. Many of the Parsees in their purple coal-hods come aboard to bid farewell to a parting friend. One of the Highlanders is going home and his comrades have brought the pipes to give him a last tune. Grief and Scotch whiskey move them finally to "play a spring and dance it round" in spite of the heat, which brings the sweat pouring down their faces. Sampans cluster about with pretty little Chinese dogs, bamboo steamer chairs, and canary birds for sale, driving a few final bargains.

. . . The bell warns them all away. I wave goodbye to my friends and to the beautiful city with the keenest regret.

. . . The fifth stage of my journey has begun under the shadow of the Union Jack.

Fifth Stage

Hong Kong vanishes in a haze of sunlight. I am desperately tired—worn out with delights. My head swims with a glorious confusion of tropic splendors, and there is no room or capacity in it for more impressions just now. I will go below. . .

It is a beautiful ship; like a fine yacht in its spacious commodiousness. Here and there hang canary cages thrilling with song. Narcissus bulbs in bowls are ablow with fluttering white flowers, and everywhere are deep-colored jars full of palms and ferns. The space assigned to me is a large, pleasant white room, from which a great square lifts up outward on the water-side, leaving me on intimate terms with the milky, jade-tinted sea. Beneath this window is a broad divan, and here, laved in tepid sea winds and soothed by rippling whispers against the ship's side, I sleep—the langorous, voluptuous sleep of the tropics; . . . sink softly into that dim warm flood where one lies drenched, submerged in unconsciousness; a flood that ebbs slowly, slowly—bearing with it all fatigue and satiety—and leaves me on the shores of life again in a pale lilac dusk glimmering with great stars. . .

Yea, verily, life is good in this magnificent equatorial world! Again I am a great sponge, absorbing beauty and delight with every pore. Everyday brings new marvels and new joys. I go to bed exhaustedly happy and wake up expectantly smiling. Everything pleases, everything amuses me; most of all perhaps the strong British atmosphere in which one finds one's self on board a P. and O. steamer. I am—with the exception of a charming little old lady from Boston, who after two years of travel in the East has suffered no diminution of her respect for the Common and Phillips Brooks—the only woman on the passenger list; so the British atmosphere has a pronounced masculine flavor; but despite even this limitation it is interesting.

The men, from captain to cook, are fine creatures. Their physical vigor is superb—such muscles! such crisply curled hair! such clear ruddy skins, white teeth, and turquoise eyes. They are flat-backed and lean-loined; they carry their huge shoulders with a lordly swagger; they possess a divine faith in themselves and in England; and they have such an astonishing collection of accents! No two of them speak alike: the burly bearded giant three places off from me at table speaks with a broad Scotch drawl; the handsome, natty little fourth officer with the black eyes and shy red face who sits opposite, in white duck from head to heel, has a bit of a Yorkshire burr on the tip of his tongue; the Ceylon tea-planter talks like a New-Yorker, and there are fully a dozen variations more between his accent and that of the tall young blond, whose fashionable Eton and Oxford inflections leave one speechless with awe and admiration of their magnificent eccentricities.

Even the menu is of daily interest, for here I become for the first time familiar with food upon which the folk of the English novels are fed. I learn to know and appreciate the Bath bun and the Scotch scone. I make the greatly-to-be-prized acquaintance of the English meat pie, including Mr. Weller's favorite "weal and 'ammer," and I recognize touching manifestations of British loyalty in the sweets christened impartially with appellations of royalty: Victoria jelly-roll, Alexandra wafers, and Beatrice tarts. Waterloo pudding is one of our favorite desserts, and other British triumphs and glories adorn the bill of fare from time to time.

. . . Sunday the Lascar crew, who have contented themselves all the week with garments of blue cotton check and red turbans, suddenly bloom and burgeon garden-wise. We are lounging in our bamboo chairs on the wide decks; the awning flutters lazily in the breeze; and we, swimming between two worlds of burning blue, are endeavoring by supreme indolence to recover from the fatigues of morning service, when this startlingly variegated vision bursts upon us: All the brown feet are bare, but the brown nether limbs are clad airily in Swiss muslin trousers, over which falls to the knee a tunic of the same material striped with fine lines of gold, silver, or scarlet thread and girdled with a vivid-hued sash, this again partly covered with a loose silk waistcoat—pink, green, or blue—glittering with spangles. Brimless hats of red and yellow straw, like inverted flat-bottomed baskets, are wrapped with many scarlet folds, and the boatswains add one more touch of splendor in their great wrought-silver buttons and yards of silver chain, from which hangs suspended the whistle of their office. I am at first inclined to suspect them of having looted the wardrobe of an odalisque, but am assured it is only the muster for the usual Sunday-morning inspection and their accustomed costume for such occasions. A brief but imposing ceremony, this. The officers exchange their white jackets for blue coats. The doctor solemnly confers with the captain, and those in imperfect hygienic condition stand on one foot in apologetic embarrassment, as they catch the piercing and reproachful glance of their commander, who passes ceremoniously down the line accompanied by the entire staff, acknowledging with condescending salute the row of brown hands lifted to the brown brows.

The boatswain sounds his whistle, the ranks are broken, and the affair is over.

Everyone goes and gets something to drink as a freshener after so much excitement and the officers change back into white jackets.

As the little fawn-eyed punkah-wallah (to put it in American, the boy who pulls the hanging fan over the table) passes me, I snatch off his turban and find his round brown head shaved smooth as my palm, except for the one lock over the brow by which Mahomet is to catch him up to heaven. He finds this liberty only an amusing condescension on my part, and smiles indulgently and shyly, following me about always afterwards with little mute services and attentions—so sweet-natured are these Eastern folk.

We sail through the blue days on a level keel. The sea does not even breathe; but it quivers in the terrible splendors of the noon with undreamable peacock radiances.

. . . The sky arches to a dome of intolerable vastness, filled with a blinding light. Hardly can its glories be borne, even in the shadow of the wide awning where one lies half the day in Indian lounging-chairs, warmed to the very heart and soaked through and through with color and light.

. . . There are no pageants of sunsets. The burning ball, undimmed by any cloud, falls swiftly and is quenched in the ocean, and after an instant of crepuscular violet the prodigious tide of light vanishes abruptly, like some vast conflagration blown out suddenly, and as suddenly succeeded by

> "The night of ebon blackness,
> Laced with lustres of starry clusters."

Then the constellations hang in the awful vault of darkness like enormous gleaming lamps trembling in suspension. And from the swart deep beneath whirl up myriads of great ghostly jewels, glittering with unearthly fires and trailing a broad waving path of spectral silver along the black waters in our wake.

. . . Every hour brings us nearer the equator, and on the morning of the 23d of December we sight Singapore, seventy miles only from the centre of heat. The waters of the harbor are curiously banded in broad lines of brilliant violet, green, and blue, each quite distinct and with no fusions of color. Against the sky line everywhere are the feathery heads of palms, and the tremendous riot of verdure upon all the hills is of a vivid, dazzling green. The vegetation is enormous, rampant, violent. . . It stands round about the place like an army with banners, ready to rush in at any breach and destroy. It contests every inch of space with man, and, aided by incessant heat and moisture, constantly wrests from him his conquests and buries them in a fury of viridescence. Seven hundred years has this City of the Lions stood, but the never-ending battle with tropic nature's lust for disintegration has left it with no monuments of its great age, no venerable buildings to testify to its antiquity. In the twelfth century Singapore was the capital of the Malayan empire, but in 1824 the British purchased it from the sultan of Jahore, scarcely more than a heap of ruins.

Only those who travel to these Eastern ports can form any adequate conception of the ability which has directed English conquest in the Orient. When they bullied the Malayan sultan into selling Singapore, they were apparently acquiring a ruinous and unimportant territory. Today this port is the entrepôt of Asian commerce, a coaling station for vessels of all countries, a deep, safe harbor for England's own ships and men-of-war, and a point from which she can command both seas. The inhabitants of her Straits Settlements number considerably more than half a million, and the exports and imports are each in value something like £10,000,000 yearly. The United States alone buys there every twelve month goods worth more than $4,000,000.

. . . It is very hot. The tall blond, who is grandson of one of the world-famous conquerors of the East, arrays himself in snowy silk and linen and dons a Terrai hat with a floating scarf; but even in this attire moisture sparkles on his rosy skin, and his yellow curls cling damply to his brow. The Ceylon tea-planter, twenty years resident in the tropics, is garbed in the ordinary costume of civilization, and apparently suffers no discomfort. Accompanied by these two and the lady from Boston, I go ashore.

Queer little square carriages, made for the most part of Venetian blinds, wait for us, drawn by disconsolate ponies the size of sheep. Conveyance in the East is a constant source of unhappiness to me. I was deprecatory with the jinrikisha men in Japan, I humbled myself before the chair-bearers of Hong Kong, and now I go and make an elaborate apology to this wretched little beast before I can reconcile it to my conscience to climb into the gharry, or let him drag me about at a gallop.

The earth beneath us is a deep red, the trees are brightly green; to the right lies a rainbow sea, and overhead a sky of burning blue. The town is every color—blinding white, azure, green, red, yellow; the houses heavy squares of lime-washed brick, mostly without windows. Interiors are gloomily cool, and more than enough of the huge fierce glare of day enters through the open door. We pass swiftly through the business part of the town, and beyond to the broad red water-road where the houses face the sea.

One is suddenly aware that the sensory nerves awake in this heat to marvellous acuteness. The eye seems to expand its iris to great size and be capable of receiving undreamed possibilities of luminosity and hue. The skin grows exquisitely sensitive to the slightest touch—the faintest movement of the air. Numberless fine under-currents of sound reach the ear, and the sense of smell is so strong that the perfumes of fruit and flowers at a great distance are penetrating as if held in the hand. One smells everything: . . . delicious hot scents of vegetation, . . . the steaming of the earth, . . . and the faint acrid odors of the many sweating bodies of workers in the sun. . .

The water-road is full of folk. Tall Hindoos go by leading little cream-white bulls with humped necks, who drag rude carts full of merchandise or fruits—pineapples, mangoes, and cocoanuts. English officials spin past in dog-carts with bare-footed muslin-clad grooms up behind, and wealthy unctuous Chinese merchants bowl about in 'rikishas. Nearly all foot-passengers are half or three-quarters naked. It is an open-air museum of superb bronzes, who, when they condescend to clothe themselves at all, drape in statuesque folds about their brown limbs and bodies a few yards of white or crimson cloth, which adorns rather than conceals. One gasps for breath as there suddenly emerges from a side street what appears to be a fat old lady coming from the bath, her gray hair knotted up carelessly and a towel as her only costume. In reality there is no cause for alarm; it is a dignified elderly Malay merchant in conventional business attire. Everyone has long hair and wears it twisted up at the nape of the neck; this, with the absence of beards and the general indeterminateness of attire, makes it difficult to distinguish sexes. The lower class of work people are black, shining, and polished as Indian idols. At work they wear only a breechcloth, but when evening comes they catch up a square of creamy transparent stuff, and by a twist or two of the wrist fold it beautifully and loosely about themselves, and with erect heads tread silently away through the dusk—slender, proud, and mysterious-eyed. The Malays are of an exquisite bronze, gleaming in the sun like burnished gold. They have full silken inky hair, very white teeth, and dress much in draperies of dull-red cotton, which makes them objects delicious to contemplate. Mingled with all these is the ubiquitous Chinaman in a pair of short loose blue breeches, his handsome muscular body shining as yellow satin.

We reach the hotel at last, its gloom, its cloistered arcades and great dark rooms pleasant enough as a refuge from the sun. The dining-room, a great vaulted hall through the centre of the building, is level with the earth, paved with stone and without doors, opening upon the veranda through three archways. Without windows, one can scarcely distinguish anything at first entrance from the glare outside; but presently we find the place full of tables of green and growing plants, and two huge punkahs waving slowly overhead, making a cooling breeze. We are served by Hindoos in garments and turbans of white muslin, who have slender melancholy brown faces, and eyes that shine through wonderful lashes with the soft gleamings of black jewels. I can scarcely eat my tiffin for delight in the enchanting pathetic beauty, the passionate grace and sadness, of the face of the lad who brings me butter in a lordly dish, the yellow rolls laid upon banana leaves, and serves me curry with a spoon made of a big pink shell.

Everyone is in lily white from head to heel, like a bride or a débutante—white duck trousers and fatigue jacket, white helmet, and white shoes.

This is the dress of two young subalterns with heads like canary birds, and the sappy red of English beef still in their cheeks, just out from home for their first experience of Eastern service. They are full of energy, interest, and enthusiasm; they order beer and beef, and mop their hot faces from time to time, listening meanwhile with profound respect to the words of their superior officer, who condescends to tiffin with them and to give them good advice. His dress is similar to theirs, save for the gold straps on his shoulders, but all the succulent English flesh has been burned off of him long ago, and left him lean, tawny, and dry. He quenches his thirst with a little iced brandy and soda, eats sparingly of curry and fruit, and seems not to feel the heat much He has no enthusiasms, he has no interests except duty and the service, and he does not think any brown or yellow person in the least pretty or pleasant.

His advice to the youngsters, while valuable, is saturninely patronizing and full of disillusionment, and one can see it falls somewhat coldly upon their youthful ardor.

. . . Mine is a huge dim apartment with a stone floor opening directly upon the lawn and into the dining-room, and has only slight jalousies for doors; but no one peers or intrudes. The bed is an iron frame; the single hard mattress is spread with a sheet, and there are no covers at all. Even the pillow is of straw. My bath-room, a lofty flagged chamber, opens into this one, and contains a big earthenware jar which the coolies fill for me three times a day, and into which I plunge to rid me of the burning heat.

. . . That night I have the most terrible adventure. Immediately I get into bed and blow out the candle, I hear what sounds like some great animal stalking about. I am cold enough now—icy, in fact. . . What can it be? . . .

They tell me tigers come over from the mainland and carry off on an average one person a day. . . This is probably a tiger. He could easily push open those blind doors and walk in! . . . He is coming towards the bed with heavy stealthy rustlings. There is not even a sheet to draw up over me. The room is hot, utterly black and still, save for the sound of those feet and the loud banging of my heart against my ribs.

. . . The hotel seems to be dead, so horribly silent it is. Has the tiger eaten everyone else already?

. . . The darkness is of no use; he can see all the better for that; so I will strike a match and at least perish in the light.

. . . As the blue flame on the wick's tip broadens I meet the gaze of a frightfully large, calm gray rat who is examining my shoes and stockings with care. He regards me with only very faint interest, and goes on with his explorations through all my possessions. He climbs the dressing-table and smells critically at my hat and gloves. . . This is almost as bad as the tiger, but as I have no intention of attacking this terrible beast and my notice appears to bore him, I blow out the candle and go to sleep, leaving him to continue those heavy rustlings which so alarmed me.

We secure an open carriage with two fine bronzes in muslin and turbans on the box, and go for a drive. The blond takes us first to call at a great white airy stone bungalow, set on a hill where resides the chief of police, another English officer clad in white and as brown and lean as are all who have seen long service here. He gives a command in Malay to his khitmagar, and we are served with tea in the Chinese fashion. No other English official can equal him in his knowledge of the Malay tongue and character, and for this reason he is sent to conduct negotiations with the sultan of Jahore whenever that potentate grows restless. None of his own suite understand what he says while there, but he always comes back with the desired concessions from the monarch and may therefore be supposed to speak the language convincingly and with eloquence. . . He has learned in his score of years in the East great gentleness of voice and manner, but underneath it is felt at once the iron texture of this man whom the natives regard with undisguised respect and fear.

From his gates the road turns towards the botanical gardens, a great park where wide red ways wind through shaven lawns and under enormous blossoming trees. Every plant one knows as exotic is here quite at home—the giant pads of the Victoria regia pave the moats with circles of emerald, and the lotus lifts its rose-flushed cups from glassy pools where swans float in shadow. We leave the carriage and pace through the translucent green twilight of the orchid houses built of wire gauze, the plants needing no protection here, where for six thousand years or so the thermometer has been ranging between seventy-five and ninety-five degrees of heat. The place is full of strange unfamiliar perfumes and grotesque blossoms, ghostly white, pallidly purple, and writhen into fantasticalities of scarlet. Our carriage waits for us in the shade of a blooming tree, and, returning, we find it sprinkled with small golden trumpets poignantly sweet.

On the way home we pass the governor's palace with its wonderful palms and bamboos, and it is upon this road that we come suddenly upon a race of brown goddesses—Klings they are called—transplanted here from Pondicherry, the fragment of India still retained by France.

. . . We pass one alone, then two, then several more going singly along the wide road shaded by enormous trees.

. . . They are very tall, with round slender limbs. . . Their garments—a long scarf of thin white wrapped firmly about the hips, drawn lightly over the bosom and crossing the back from shoulder to waist—but half conceal beneath the semi-transparent drapery the fine outline of breast and hip, clear and firm as ancient statues, and warmly brown with a curious faint bloom—almost as of a grape—upon the skin. As they go forward, lightly and fleetly, on their slim bare feet they have the proud, upstanding grace of palms, and with a strange sinuous motion make all their heavy anklets and bangles tinkle like little bells and a wave of fluent movement stir their garments from throat to heel. The ripples of their hair, drawn back from the broad brown brows and knotted in silken abundance at the nape, glitter like polished jet, and the fine, haughty, dark features lit with little points of gold—tiny studs set in the high nostrils and the upper rims of the little ears.

. . . As we pass, they raise languid great eyes of unfathomable blackness with a gaze half mystical, half sensual, that stirs the heart with a vague sudden pain of yearning and sadness. . . It is a race famous throughout India for the astonishing beauty of its women; but as they will not allow themselves to be photographed, I can get no record of their loveliness.

. . . Half-past four! The ship is about to sail. We have wandered through the shops and museums, and have returned once more to our old quarters. Tiny canoes cluster about the vessel, full of beautiful shells of which one can buy a boat-load for a dollar. Other canoes hold small Malays ranging from three to seven years of age, all naked save for the merest rag of a breechcloth, all pretty as little bronze curios, and all shouting in shrill chorus for coins. A few shillings changed into the native currency procures a surprising number of small pieces of money, which we fling into the clear water. They plunge over after these with little splashings like frogs, and wiggle down swiftly to the bottom, growing strange and wavering of outline and ghostly green as they sink. They are wonderfully quick to seize the glinting coin before it touches the sands below, and come up wet, shining, and showing their white teeth. We play at this game until the whistle blows, and then sail away, leaving the blond waving his handkerchief to us from the shore.

An hour later we are still steaming near the palm-fringed coast. There is a sudden cry and struggle forward—a naked yellow body with manacled hands shoots outward from the ship's side and disappears in a boiling circle of foam. A Chinese prisoner, being transported to Penang, has knocked down his guards and taken to the water. The engines are reversed and a life-buoy thrown overboard, but he does not appear. After what seems a great lapse of time, a head shows a long distance away and moves rapidly towards the shore. Evidently he has slipped his handcuffs and can swim. A boat is lowered full of Lascars very much excited, commanded by the third officer, a ruddy young fellow—calm and dominant. They pursue the head, but it has covered more than half the distance, some two miles, between us and the shore before it is overtaken. There is some doubling back and forth, an oar is raised in menace, and the fugitive submits to be pulled into the boat. I am standing by the gangway when he returns. He is a fine, well-built young fellow. His crime is forgery, and he is to be turned over to the native authorities against whom he has offended. Their punishments are terrible: prisoners receive no food, and must depend upon the memories and mercies of the charitable.

. . . One of the Lascars holds him by the queue as he mounts the steps. He is wet and chilled, and has a face of stolid despair.

They take him forward, and I see him no more.

. . . It is Christmas Day—still very hot; and off to our right are to be seen from time to time the bold purple outlines of the coasts of Sumatra. The ship is decorated with much variegated bunting, and the servants assume an air of languid festivity; but most of us suffer from plaintive reminiscences of home and nostalgia. There is a splendid plum-cake for dinner, with a Santa Claus atop, huddled in sugar furs despite the burning heat. We pull Christmas crackers, as in the holidays at home, and from their contents I am loaded with paste jewels and profusely provided with poetry in brief segments and of an enthusiastically amatory nature.

. . . Penang.—Its peaks shoot sharply up into the blue air 2000 feet, wrapped in a tangle of prodigious verdure to their very tops, enormous palm forests fringing all the shore. The ship anchors some distance from the docks, and will remain but a few hours. We are ferried to land in crazy sampans, the only alternative from out-rigger canoes—a narrow trough set on a round log and kept upright by a smaller floating log connected with the boat by bent poles. Only a native, a tight-rope walker, or a bicyclist would trust himself to these.

. . . The same crowd of Hindoos, Malays, and Chinese.

Little girls of twelve or thirteen stand about with their own children in their arms. They have been wives for a year or two. Very pretty they are, miniature women fully formed; the babies fat and brown and nearly as large as the mothers.

A gharry and another pitiful little horse take us towards the gardens and the famous waterfall. The road skirts the town and intersects lagoons, where Malay houses of cocoanut thatch stand upon piles like ancient lake dwellings. They live over this stagnant water by preference, and apparently suffer no harm. Farther on, where the ground rises, are the huge stone bungalows of English officials and rich Chinese merchants, the entrance to the grounds of the latter adorned with ornate doors and guarded by carved monsters, curiously colored.

We overtake a Chinese funeral winding towards the cemetery, all the mourners clad in white. The coffin, of unpainted wood, is so heavy and so large that twenty pall-bearers are required to carry it. It is a most cheerful cortége. No one seems in the least downcast or dispirited by this bereavement—death is accepted by that race with the same stolid philosophy as are the checkered incidents of life.

. . . The road turns and sweeps into the palm forest. Innumerable slender, silver-gray columns soar to an astonishing height—a hundred feet or more—bearing at the top a wide feathery crown where the big globes of the cocoanuts hang, green and gold.

Up there, in the tops of the palms, flows a dazzling flood of light, and as the faint warm wind waves the huge drooping fans we catch flashes of flaming blue; but below we are in shadow and cannot feel the wind's breath. A profound green twilight reigns here, with something, I know not what, of holy sadness and awe amid these silent gray aisles—delicate, lofty, still—such as might move the heart in an ancient minister's calm pillared silences. . .

Our guide, a brown lad of ten, stands on the carriage-step clinging to the door, and chatters fluently in tangled and intricate English, of which he is obviously inordinately vain. At the garden entrance he makes us dismount, vehicles not being allowed inside, and leads us along the broad, beautifully tended paths. The garden lies between two very lofty cone-shaped peaks and is as well kept and full of tropical blossoms and verdure as are all the others we have seen. The boy stops to show me in the grass tiny fronds of the sensitive-plant, that shudder away from his rude little finger with a voluntary movement startling to see in a plant.

We hear the rushing speech of waters calling loudly in the hills, but see nothing save the mountain's garments of opulent verdure. A path zigzags sharply upward through the trees and vine labyrinth, and by this the boy leads the way with the speed and agility of a goat. We pant along in his wake, barely keeping him in sight.

It is frightfully hot in here among the trees. The atmosphere is a steam bath, and the moisture pours down our faces as we spring from stone to stone and corkscrew back and forth, deafened by the vociferations of the fall, but catching no glimpse of it. Exhausted, gasping, streaming with perspiration, we finally emerge upon a plateau high on the peak's side and are suddenly laved in that warm wind that stirred the palm fronds. . . At our feet is a wide, quivering green pool, crossed by a frail bridge; from far above leaps down to us a flood of glittering silver that dashes the emerald pool into powdery foam, races away under the bridge, and springs again with a shout into the thickets below. We lose sight of it amid the leaves, but can hear its voice as it leaps from ledge to ledge down to the valley and is silenced at last in the river.

A tiny shrine built here at the side of this first pool is tended by a thin melancholy-eyed young priest, who lives alone at this great height, his only companions the ceaseless bruit of the waters and the little black elephant-headed god in the shrine. He bears a spot of dried clay upon his forehead—a token of humility. At his morning devotions he dips his hand in the water, then in the dust, touches it upon his brow, and wears this sign of submission all day. I lay a piece of money upon the altar, and in return am given a handful of pale, perfumed pink bells that grow upon the mountain-side, and are the only sacrifice offered to the little black god. The priest will have me remove my hat and decorate my hair with the flowers in the fashion in which his countrywomen wear them, and is pleased when I comply.

. . . Back again through the steaming woods and the palm aisles; then the ship once more, and our faces are turned towards Ceylon.

Sixth Stage

It is a five days' run from Penang to the island of Ceylon; the shop's company has dwindled to a handful, and time hangs heavily upon us. We are reduced, for lack of other occupations, to an undue interest in the ship's menagerie.

The pretty little fifth officer has a monkey—a surreptitious monkey, not allowed to members of the staff—and at such time as the stern seniors are on duty we amuse ourselves fearfully and secretly with his antics.

A tiny Methuselah-faced simian, regarding all his human cousins with loathing suspicion, but to be placated with raisins. A small shivering, chattering captive, dancing to amuse his jailers, with a grin of hate on his sorrowful weazened countenance. At other times, while the powers that be look on, the Fifth and I sport ostentatiously with two gorgeous and permissible cockatoos, whom we find, like most things permissible, dull and uninteresting.

The consul to Bangkok—a slim, brown gentleman with a soft, languid voice and tiny feet—is carrying home a family of Siamese cats; white, with tawny legs and fierce blue eyes; uncanny beasts with tigerish ways. They live in the fo'castle in company with an impulsive Chinese puppy of slobberingly affectionate disposition; and their prowling, long-legged behavior gets upon his nerves most terribly. He is too manly a little person to hurt them, and his only refuge is an elaborate pretence of not seeing; even when they rub against his nose he gazes abstractedly off into space and firmly refuses to be aware of their existence.

. . . The doctor has two families of felines—one a respectable tortoise-shell British matron, absorbed with the cares of a profuse maternity, and the other a splendid Persian lady, madly jealous of the division in her owner's affections. He purchased her from a native on the wharves at Bombay—smelling of violet powder and with a gold thread around her neck—a theft from some zenana, and wild with several days' starvation and bad treatment. She has not, however, forgotten the ways of her odalisque mistress, and is greedy, luxurious, indolent, and bad-tempered. If the doctor dares, after touching the kittens, to caress her without having previously washed his hands, her keen nose detects his perfidy; she flies into a fury, claws, spits, rages, and finally rushes up

ELIZABETH BISLAND

into the rigging to sulk until he grovels with apologies and holds out seductive visions of dinner.

. . . It is eight o'clock in the morning. The ship is anchored off the coast of Ceylon.

We arrived late last night; sailing into the harbor by the light of great tropical stars and the planet gleams of a pharos shining from the tall clock-tower of Colombo. Already many ships lie in the narrow roadstead, and it requires the fine art of navigation to slip our boat's huge bulk into her berth between two of these and make her fast to her own particular buoy. The pilot came aboard just outside, and it is his firm hand that jams her nose up to within three hairs' breadth of the vessel in front, holds her there with a grip of iron, and with cautious screw-revolutions swings her into line with her heels in the very face of the Australian mail-ship—arrived a few hours earlier.

Then the entire passenger list—on deck for the last half-hour, aiding the pilot by holding its breath—sighs relievedly and joyously, and goes below in a body to recuperate on brandy and soda.

. . . I linger a moment in the darkness to smell the fragrance of the night, moved by the vast flowings of a warm sweet wind. Seafarers of other days told of these perfumes of the Spice Island filling their sails far out at sea, but the coal smoke of the modern ship deadens the nostril of the modern traveller, and fills his heart with naughty doubts of the veracity of the Ancient Mariner. Natheless there are in the mountain forests of Ceylon strange, treeless, lake-like expanses of aromatic lemon grass from which the winds come heavy with intoxicating scents. . . I fancy I can detect faint delicious savors in the air, and that night— sleeping with open port-holes—I dream of perfumes.

. . . I am up early to have the first possible view of an island so like to Paradise that Adam was first banished to this place that he might not feel too sharply in the beginning his loss and the contrast.

Upon Adam's Peak—a soaring pinnacle seven thousand feet high, of which we caught a glimpse yesterday while still far at sea—stood the father of men and wept his lost Eden, for which even Ceylon might not console him; the bitter rain of this immeasurable grief trickling down the mountain-side into the rocks, the rivers, the sea, and the sands, where it is found today as clear shining gems and pearls like tears. It was upon this peak that, having clothed himself in the skins of beasts, he shred abroad to the winds the first green garments that hid his primal nakedness, and these, scattered far and wide by the breeze, sprang up in spice plants—so ambrosial a potency had even the leaves of the trees in Paradise.

Very like in the early morning looks this island of jewels, of flowers, and palms to the long-lost heavenly gardens. It floats upon a smooth, nacreous waste of waters, under a sky of pale warm violet, veiled in a dawn-mist faint and mysterious as dreams. Beyond the massive breakwater of our straitened harbor curve the rims of white beaches frilled with foam, where palms lean over to look at themselves in a sea of green mother-of-pearl. Inland the purple distances rise into lofty outlines deliciously softened and rounded by their enormous garment of verdure. The prospect is very pleasing. One is prepared to condone any possible vileness of the inhabitants.

It is very hot. The thermometer even at this hour (it is the last day of December) registers 80°; but it is less oppressive than at Singapore, where one seemed to be breathing tepid water rather than air.

A long wharf juts out into the harbor with a custom-house at its landward end. We pause here to exchange some civilities concerning the weather, and pass on with our luggage unmolested, so soothing and plentiful a lack of curiosity have these officials in British ports.

. . . The soil is red—bright red—the color of ground cinnabar. Not "liver-colored," as the earth seemed to the ancient Northmen, but deep-tinted as if soaked with dragon's blood, of which antiquity believed cinnabar to be made. A broad street, fringed with grass and tulip-trees, goes inland, and on either side are massive white buildings with arched and pillared arcades. . . The vividness of color here is astounding—brilliant, intense, like the colors of precious stones. We doubt the evidence of our senses—doubt the earth *can* be so red, the sea and sky so blue. . . It is a miracle wrought by the ineffable luminosity of the Eastern day! One's very flesh tingles with an ecstasy of pleasure in this giant effulgence of color, as might a musician's who should hear the prodigious vibrations of some undreamably colossal harp.

The Grand Oriental Hotel lies to the right of this road, near the water; big and glaringly white without, cool and shadowy within. Ships from India, China, and Australia have just arrived, and the place is crowded. The clack of many heels rings on the stone floor of the arcade, which opens upon an inner flowery court, where also look out the windows of the sleeping-rooms above, veiled by delicate transparent straw mattings—waving softly in and out in the little hot breezes, giving treacherous glimpses now and again of a pretty dishevelled head and tumbled white draperies... The arcade is full of British folk—Australians and Anglo-Indians, passing to and fro to the dining-room, to the stairs, to the front entrance. Handsome, as an Anglo-Saxon crowd of the well-to-do is apt to be—tall, florid men in crisp white linen and white Indian helmets; tall, slim, well-poised girls in white muslin, with a delicious fruit-like pink in their cheeks, brought there by the heat, which curls their blond hair in damp rings about their brows and white necks. And tall, imposing British matrons, with something of the haughtiness of old Rome in their bearing—the mothers and wives of conquerors.

Our rooms are at the end of a long corridor, looking on the street. They are carpetless and uncurtained, their dim twilight being sifted from the burning glare without through green mattings hung at the windows. Before my door sits my own particular servant, detailed to wait upon this bedroom. Similar servants are stationed along the corridor in front of their respective charges. This attendant seems never to go away, for at whatever hour I need him he is there. Even at night he does not desert his post, unrolling a rug and sleeping where he sat all day... A curious creature—of a sex not easily to be determined. Mild-browed and woman-eyed, with long, rippling black hair knotted at the back and kept smooth with a tortoise-shell band comb, the brown femininities of his face disappear at the chin in a short close-curled black beard. He is full-chested as a budding girl, but clothes himself to the waist in shirt, coat, and waistcoat, the slender male hips being wrapped in a white skirt that falls to the ankles.

He is, however, an eminently agreeable person. The gentle and confiding affection of his manner leaves speechless with joyful amazement the humbled victim of the harsh and haughty tyranny of the American servant-girl. He not only executes orders with noiseless despatch, but receives them with a little reverence of the slim fingers to the brow, and a look in his lustrous eyes of such sweet eagerness to serve that my heart is melted within me. I find myself asking for hot water with the coo of a sucking dove; I demand butter at table in the mild tones of a wind-harp, and converse with the guide in a manner I might naturally assume to a beloved younger sister. This atmosphere of loving-kindness is that of Paradise. It expands the heart with unreflecting happiness, and makes man, even servant-man, my brother. Discreetly I refrain from too close examination, lest this refreshing mirage resolve on nearer view to blank and desert indifference, and for these two days I choose to live in a sunshine of reciprocal amenities.

. . . It is the sacred and beautiful hour of tiffin. The dining-room is as white, cool, and nobly plain as a Greek temple; long and very lofty—reaching to the roof—the second story opening upon it in an arched and balustraded clere-story. Two punkahs of gold-colored stuff wave above us. On one side we look upon the arcaded court, and through the heavy-arched veranda upon the hot gorgeousness of color outside. Bowls of tropical flowers are set on each table, and under the salt-cellars and spoons at the corners are laid large leaves of curious lace-like pattern, freaked with splashes of red and yellow. More of the fawn-eyed men with long hair serve us, and the assemblage gathered here for the moment is a remarkable one. Near the door sits a good-looking young man, accompanying a party of blond girls in smart frocks. It is Wordsworth's grandson, and the owner of Rydal Mount. At the table next him is a stern, lean soldier with a melancholy face—the Lord Chelmsford in whose African campaign the Prince Imperial was killed and the English suffered a hideous butchery, surprised by the savages. On the other side of the room is a young man with a heavy blond countenance—Dom Leopoldo Agostino and half a dozen things more, who has just met here, in his voyage round the world in a Brazilian war-ship, the news of his grandfather Dom Pedro's dethronement and exile. The captain of the ship dares not continue the cruise in the face of peremptory cables from the new government, and the young man is suddenly marooned here, with all his luggage and attendants, under the protection of the British lion, who has always a friendly paw for *les rois en exil*. Near us is a man with a bulging orehead and a badly-fitting frock-coat of black broadcloth—a noted mesmerist from America, with a little Texan wife fantastically gowned; she, poor soul, having a picturesque instinct, but no technique. Beyond him is a man of middle age, with a fine, saturnine countenance, lean and bold as the head of Cæsar, and an air of great distinction. It is Sir William Robinson, an Irishman, a well-known composer, and a colonial governor. Beside him sits Sir Henry Wrenfordsly, a colonial chief-justice. At their table is Lady Broome, a tall, handsome woman with a noble outline of brow and head. Under the title of Lady Barker, she is the author of many well-known and delightful books on life in the Antipodes. Sir Napier Broome is also tall and handsome, and is on his way home from an Australian governorship.

. . . In the arcade that faces on the street are native shops—tiny cells full of basket-work, wrought brass, laces, jewels; carvings in ivory, ebony, and tortoise-shell; India shawls and silks, Cingalese silver-work, and such small trinkets and souvenirs best calculated to lure the shy rupee from its lair in the traveller's pocket. Most of these shops are kept by Moormen—large, yellow, unpleasant-looking persons in freckled calico petticoats, heads shaven quite clean and covered with a little red basket too small for the purpose. They inspire carking disgust and suspicion by their craven oiliness; their wares for the most part not worth a tenth of the sums asked.

Jewels are to be had at astonishing rates—cat's-eyes and moon-stones being sold carelessly by the handful. The arcade is full of itinerant merchants who carry their stock of precious stones—sometimes quite valuable—tied up in a dingy rag, disposing of them by methods of barter quite unique. Twenty times the proper value is demanded, and poignant outcries of bitter astonishment greet the unbelievably meagre offer of the Sahib, who should be as father and as mother to the merchant, but who proffers him only an insult. The rag is tied up in wounded amazement half a dozen times before a compromise suggests itself. Innocent joy dawns on the vender's countenance—chance shall settle it. Will the Sahib toss to decide whether he shall give for this beautiful cat's-eye two pounds or five? The original sum asked having been twenty, the Sahib sees signs of relenting, and consents to try the turn of the coin. The toss is fairly conducted, and whether he wins or loses the importunate merchant appears content, as in any case he makes a profit. This warfare of barter being as the breath of his nostrils, he is reduced to the verge of tears by the heartless conduct of those who pay him his price without protest or haggling. He himself is given to discomposing *coups de commerce*—offering a bit of tortoise-shell carving for five pounds, and accepting the five shillings proffered in derision with breath-snatching alacrity.

. . . A snake-charmer is squatting in the dust before the hotel, performing feats of juggling: playfully depositing an egg in one ear, and in a moment picking it, with a sweet smile of surprise, out of the other—or seeming to do it.

Tossing into the air a cocoanut, which obviously he has no present use for, as it remains up there out of sight for a time while he goes on with his other tricks, until we are suddenly aware of its lying beside him, and cannot recall whether it was there from the first or not.

—Rubbing his egg between open, outstretched palms until they meet and the egg is rubbed away to nothing at all, and restoring it to existence by rotary movements of his palms in the opposite direction.

Simple feats that are surprising, because he is quite naked save for a turban and a loin-cloth, and has no aids to his art but the brown cotton bag in which he carries his few properties, and a small flat basket where a cobra is coiled. But his hands are marvellously deft and supple— the hands of an old race, slim, pliant, well modelled, and exquisitely dexterous.

—He takes off the cover of the snake basket, the reptile within lying sullenly sluggish until a rap over the head induces him to lift himself angrily, puff out his throat, and make ready to strike. But his master is playing a low, monotonous tune on a tiny bamboo flute, with his eyes fastened upon the snake's eyes, and swaying his nude body slowly from side to side.

The serpent stirs restlessly, and flickers his wicked, thin red tongue; but the sleepy tune drones on and on, and the brown body moves to and fro—to and fro. Presently the serpent begins to wave softly, following the movements of the man's body and with his eyes fixed on the man's eyes, and so in time sinks slowly in a languid heap of relaxed folds. . . The music grows fainter, fainter; dies away to a breath—a whisper— ceases. The man hangs the helpless inert serpent—drunk with the insistent low whine of the flute—about his bare neck and breast, and comes forward to beg a rupee for his pains.

. . . We—the Lady from Boston, her son, the Ceylon tea-planter, and myself—hire a guide and carriage and go for a drive. Through the town, past the tall clock-tower whose flashing light showed our path last night; past the banks and the haunts of the money-changers—"shroffs" with fat, yellow, hook-nosed faces, clad in crisp white buttoned with gold, and with great circles of thin gold wire in their ears and black-and-gold head-dresses on their smooth-shaven crowns.—Past the beautiful sickle-shaped beach of Galle Face, and then inland along the shadowy dank roads under the heavy green vault of the multitudinous palms— cocoanut palms (forty millions of these, the guide says), Palmyra palms, from which the heady palm-wine is made; Kitul palms that yield sugar and sago; talipot palms, upon whose papyrus-like leaves were inscribed the sacred writings—Mahawanso—five hundred years before Christ, and preserved twenty-two centuries at Wihares; and the areca palm, that gives the nuts the natives chew with their betel leaves. We pass banyan-trees with roots like huge pythons coiling through the grass, and down-dropped stems from the far-spreading branches, making dim, leafy cloisters. Breadfruit-trees, monster ferns, pools full of lotus plants, and orchids growing almost as freely as weeds.

The guide, a gentlemanly person in a skirt, has the usual mane of rippling hair bound in a sleek knot at the nape, and at my request he untwists this and lets it fall far below his waist in silky black waves— restoring it in a moment by a quick turn of the wrist to its former neat compactness. He has never seen a hair-pin, and the gift of one of mine childishly delights and amuses him. He thrusts it in and out of his hair, and finally fastens it upon a string of queer charms and fetiches worn in his bosom.

He wraps for me a bit of areca nut with a paste of wet lime in a leaf of the betel pepper, and bids me chew it. Instantly my mouth is full of a liquid red as blood, and tongue and lips are shrivelled with a sharp aromatic astringent resembling cloves. I hasten to spit it out, but all day my lips are still hot and acrid from the brief experiment. The entire population of Ceylon are wedded to the betel habit, save the servants of Europeans who object to the unpleasant vampire red of the stained mouth and corroded teeth. It harms no more than tobacco, and the natives prefer it even to food. From time to time along the road we come upon old women sitting upon the earth with little stores of nuts, lime, and betel leaves spread before them for the refreshment of the wayfarer.

. . . "Mem Sahib," says the guide, touching his brow with his fingers, and giving me one of those smiling black glances—"you are my father and my mother. Will you that we go to the cinnamon gardens?" . . . And on the way he feeds upon ripe mangoes that have a reddish custard-like pulp, sweetly musky in flavor.

From among the cinnamon bushes growing without order in the white sand, and breathing faint odors in the steaming heat, starts out a lean, naked lad begging for alms. He is not to be shaken off, following in a leaping dance with flying hair and a white-toothed smile, clapping his elbows against his ribs with a noise like castanets, and rattling his bones together loudly and merrily as though a skeleton pranced after us through the dust; so that we are fain to end the exhibition of his unique powers with a few coins.

In the museum that stands in the cinnamon gardens we find Eden's serpents—the reverse side of this painted island paradise. The dull, venomous cobra in his spotted cowl; clammy, strangling folds of long pythons; twenty-foot sharks with horrid semi-circular hedges of teeth—the wolves of these pearl-sown seas—and endless stinging, biting, poisoning creatures wrought into wanton bizarreries by nature in some mood of cynical humorousness. Here are also the uncouthly hideous masks of the old devil dancers; great gold ornaments, splendid robes, and the ingeniously murderous weapons of this mild-mannered race, who count in their history twenty-six kings done treacherously to death. In other rooms are the stuffed skins of beautiful birds, huge mammals, and collections of rich-colored butterflies and moths—all very hardly defended from the ravenous tropical disintegration, as fierce and implacable as the productiveness is profuse. It is a nature that devours her own children; creating with a furious fecundity, and consuming all her creations with insatiable, relentless voracity.

. . . A long road among palms. Palm-thatched huts, with idle brown folk, half naked, dreaming in the heat. A door in a ruinous wall—shaven-headed priests in yellow robes—then a dim temple, with tall gods whose heads reach stiffly up to the roof.

Penetrating jasmine odors from altars heaped with stemless pink blossoms, and the Lord Buddha reclining on his elbow, drowsing in the hot semi-darkness among the stifling scents. He is forty feet long, painted a coarse vivid crimson and yellow, but his flat wooden face is fixed in the same passive, low-lidded calm that we saw upon it when he sat on his lotus among the Japanese roses, or listened in his tiny mountain shrine at Penang to loud voices of the waters. A Nirvana peace, undisturbed by passions or pity. . . dreaming eternal dreams in the hot, perfumed gloom. About the walls are painted in archaic frescoes the pains and toils of his fifty incarnations of Buddhahood, through which he attained at last to this immortal peace. Vishnu and Siva are the tall gods that stand by the doorway, for to these he gives room and shares with them his altar flowers.

A swarm closes about us as we emerge, crying for alms, and not to be ignored or beaten off. They have roused themselves from their lethargy in the simmering gloom of the palm-shaded huts, and throng clamorous and insistent for the charity the Lord Buddha has enjoined, impeding our footsteps and clinging to the carriage. Old women hold out the little soft hands of the dimpled naked babies they carry on their hip. They themselves are hideous, repulsive hags—mere wrinkled, disgusting rags of humanity, with red-stained, toothless mouths; and this at forty years. The young women are plump and pretty, with a discontented knot in their brows, and hopeless, peevish mouths—femininity being a perplexing and bitter burden in the East. Small brown imps, naked as Adam, save for a heavy silver necklace hung about their fat, little stomachs, cling to our knees and use their fine eyes with a coquette's conscious power, smilingly seducing the coin out of our pockets.

. . . It is the last night of the old year, and the dining-hall has been converted into a ballroom. The men, all in white, with gay sashes about their middle, are circling languidly with pretty English girls in their arms. A high, warm wind whirls through the veranda and flutters the draperies of the lookers-on.

The woman from Texas, in a fearful and wonderful costume, that casts a slight but comprehensive glance at the modes of three centuries and muddles them all, is tossing her powdered head and flirting shrilly with the soft-voiced governor with the Cæsar face. A handsome ruddy old soldier with gray hair is moodily mounting guard over his three lank-elbowed partnerless daughters, whose plump and pleasing mamma is frolicking jovially about, clasped to the bosom of all Ceylon's military ornaments. Wordsworth's grandson, who looks as if designed to an order by Du Maurier, is waltzing, lazily graceful, with one of the smartly gowned blond girls. . .

Faint rhythmic breathings of the music come to my chamber window. The night is hot and silent—full of musky perfumes, of vague ghostly stirrings, of "old unhappy far-off things," that move one with poignant mysterious memories of the dense tropical darkness, with its silent, flitting figures—full of the glimmering, bewildered phantoms of passions and pains that perished centuries ago.

. . . Morning!—The new year is coming in a beautiful green dawn. A chrysoberyl sky, translucent golden green, a misty green sea, and an ocean of feathery green plumes tossing noiselessly, as with a great silent joy, in the morning wind.

I have sprung out of bed to receive a letter—my first one from home. A few lines, scrawled on the other side of the world, that I lean from the window to read in the faint early light. How beautiful they make the new year seem!—Whatever this coming year will contain of grief and rebuffs, at least it has begun with one good moment, and for that it is well to be grateful. . .

Seventh Stage

At Ceylon the Australian mail-ship Britannia waits for us. She is one of the enormous Peninsular and Oriental vessels built in the Jubilee year, and is on her way home to England.

. . . Here again farewells: to the dear little old lady from Boston and to my kind and charming friend the Ceylon tea-planter, who has placed me under an endless debt of gratitude by his many courtesies. It is four o'clock in the afternoon of the 1st of January when we swing out of the harbor and direct our course towards Africa.

The height of luxury is achieved on these Peninsular and Oriental steamships. No steerage travel being provided for, space is not stinted to first-class passengers, and saloons, decks, and bedrooms are ample and handsome. The ship's company, Australians on their way home to England, have made themselves thoroughly at home for the six weeks' cruise. Their rooms they have hung with photographs and drapery and bits of bric-à-brac, and on deck each one has a long bamboo lounging-chair, a little table, and a tea-service for that beautiful ceremony of five-o'clock tea—all being made possible by the fact that the sea is smooth as glass and the decks level as a drawing-room floor. Courtesies are exchanged in the form of invitations to this afternoon tea. Three times a week the band plays for dancing on deck; tableaux, private theatricals, and fancy balls fill the evenings, and in the afternoons the after-part of the ship is lively with games of cricket.

The principal personage on board is Miss Ethel Roma Detmold, aged two and a half years, and familiarity known as Baby Detmold. There are other infants aboard, but merely "the common or garden" baby, not to be mentioned with this blue-and-gold girl child who sparkles out upon us a morning vision in a white frock and an enigmatic smile. The entire male force of the ship is her slave, and trailing about after her, humbly suing for favors she is most chary in granting, she possessing already the secret of power over her kind in an airy, joyous indifference to anyone's attentions and services, which we therefore—with the curious perversity of human nature—persist in thrusting upon her.

All women are not borne free and equal. . . There is some subtle force in this tiny turquoise-eyed coquette which will secure for her without effort, her life through, devotion other women may not win with endless sacrifices or oceans of tears. Even the cook's pet chicken, who flies from everyone else, allows himself to be hauled about by one leg or squeezed violently to her youthful bosom, and, far from protesting, looks foolishly flattered by the notice of this imperious cherub.

. . . Always above and below us it is intensely blue, hot, and calm. Flights of film-winged fishes rise from our path and flit away like flocks of sea-sparrows. Sometimes a whale blows up a column of shining spray and leaves a green wake to show his hidden path. But nothing marks the passing of the hours save the coming and going of light.

When the azure blossom of the day dies in irised splendors, rosy clouds float up over the horizon's edge like wandering fairy islands drifting at will in a golden world—vanishing when the moon appears.

. . . Magical white nights of ineffable stillness and purity fade into the blaze of daffodil dawns. . . Time goes by in lotus dreams that have no memory of a past or reckoning of a future till we wake suddenly, and find anchor cast in the gulf of Aden.

. . . Red barren masses of stone, broken and jagged like

"An old lion's cheek teeth."

. . . An astonishing aridity everywhere, all the more startling by contrast with the fierce verdure of the lands we have last seen.

Not a drop of rain has fallen here in three years, and no green thing lives in the place. Even the tawny hills rot and fall to dust in the terrible desiccation. The earth is an impalpable dun powder that no roots could grasp; the rocks are seamed, cracked, and withered to the heart;—the dust and bones of a dead land.

. . . As a coaling station and harbor from which war-ships may guard the entrance of the Red Sea, Aden is valuable; and therefore, like Hong Kong, Singapore, Penang, Ceylon—like everything much worth having in this part of the world—it is an English possession. There are wharves of heavy masonry; the governor's residence, a verandaed bungalow shut in with green persiennes, standing on a little eminence some distance back from the water; and one narrow street of heavy white stone houses with flat roofs, fringing the shore.

A carriage is hired to convey us to the Tanks—the only bit of sight-seeing to be done at Aden.

These Tanks are of unknown antiquity and are variously attributed to Solomon, the Queen of Sheba, the Arabs, and—as a last guess—to the Phœnicians.

Historians, when in doubt, always accuse the Phœnicians.

In this rainless region, where water falls only at intervals of years, it was necessary to collect and preserve it all, and *someone* built among the hills huge stone basins with capacity of hundreds of thousands of gallons. These basins are quite perfect still, though the name of the faithful builder thereof has long ago perished.

The road winds upward from the sea to a barrier of rocks, and pierces them with a black echoing pass two hundred feet high and fifteen wide, where the English fortifications lie—a place to be held by twenty men against an army.

Here we find Tommy Atkins again, still clad in white linen from top to toe and still rosily swaggering.

On the other side of the wall of hills is the town, a motley assemblage of more flat-topped stone dwellings, all lime-washed as white as snow. In the midst is a well where women in flowing drapery, with tall jars, draw water as if posing for Bible illustrations; and a camel market in which fifty or more of the brown, ungainly beasts have been relieved of their burdens and lain down for the night—doubled into uncomfortable heaps and bubbling and moaning with querulous discontent.

We rattle through the silent, dusty town and find beyond it a garden where a dozen feeble trees have by constant watering been induced to grow as high as our heads, but appear discouraged and drooping and ready to give up the effort at any moment. Behind these are the irregular bowls of masonry set in the clefts at the foot of the rocks, and stretching enormous thirsty mouths open to the arid hills and rainless sky. They are terraced down the sides—steps by which the retreating water can be followed—but happily the place is independent of them now—with a condensing-engine and the inexhaustible supply of the sea. . .

Night is coming on. There is a crystalline luminosity in this dray air that the vanished sun leaves faintly golden-green. Every fold and crevice of the red rock wall over-flows with intense violet shadows that still are full of light. There is no evening mistiness of vision; the little flat white town, the shore, the turbaned figures moving to and fro in the streets, the ships afloat on the glassy sea, the tawny outline of the rocks—all standing out with keen clearness through the deepening of the twilight.

. . . So might have looked some Syrian evening of long ago; and, as if to answer the thought, there slowly lifts itself above the crest of the hills, in the green dusk, a huge white planet—the Star in the East! . . .

The dusk has vanished when we reach the wharf—

"At one stride comes the dark,"

and suddenly, in an instant, innumerable glittering hosts rush into the heavens with a wild, astonishing splendor, startling as the blare of trumpets. . . unimaginable myriads, unreckonable millions.

And as our oars dip, the water answers with equal multitudes of wan sea-stars that whirl and wimple through the flood.

. . . Later, when the silver fire of a full moon, by whose light one can read and see colors, has swallowed up this glittering pageant, we go again to the Tanks, passing on the route a loaded train of camels lurching away to the desert through the black shadows of the pass, and, stepping beside them, lean, swarthy Arabs, draped statelily in white— such a caravan as might have gone down into Egypt to buy corn from Pharoah four thousand years ago—nothing in the interval changed in anyway.

Our footsteps and our voices echo in hollow whispers from the empty Tanks and the mysterious shadows of the hills, though we walk lightly and speak softly, awed by the vast calm radiance of the African night.

Other than this it is very silent in this dead and desert spot; not a leaf to rustle, not an insect to cry—and even the sea has no speech.

The world grows dreamlike and unreal in the white silence.

We should feel no surprise to come suddenly among the rocks upon a gaunt Hebrew with wild eyes, clothed in skins, and wrestling in the desert with the old unsolvable riddles of existence—a prophet whose scorching words should wither away in one terrible instant all the falsities and frivolities of our lives, leaving us gaping aghast in the awful visage of Truth.

. . . Nor should we start to hear the thin, high voice of a wandering lad with the shadow of a crown above his brow, who should come chanting psalms of longing for green pastures and still waters.

It is a night and a place for such things as these.

. . . The town, beyond which shines the silver sea, is white as pearls in the moonlight, with here and there a yellow gleam from a lamp through an open door. The population is gathered in the square playing dominoes and games of chance at little tables and drinking coffee—liquor being forbidden to these Mohometans.—Bearded Arabs with delicate features and grave, sad eyes, who fold their white bornouses about them with a wonderful effect of dignity; and more jovial and half-naked negroes of every tint and race—from Zanzibar, the Soudan, Abyssinia. The Soudanese are fine, stalwart animals—fighting-men, all—stripped to the waist, shining like polished ebony, with beardless mouths full of ivory teeth, and long wool combed straight out and vividly red—made so by being plastered down for a week under a coat of lime. Egypt and England know well how these men fight; yet when I lean forward and take into my hand the little case of camel-skin containing verses from the Koran, hanging on the muscular black breast of one of these gigantic Africans, he laughs the same mellow, amiable laugh I should hear from a negro at home on the plantation, did I show a like familiarity and interest.

. . . Our way home lies through a reverberant tunnel beneath the fort, where we meet more camels still with that same lounging stride, still with that air of evangelical superiority to a wicked world, and still making, with closed mouths, those suppressed moans of wounded feeling.

The port is fast asleep. In the distance a man-of-war is slowly steaming out of the harbor on its way to the lower coast to over-awe the Portuguese making futile protests against English domination in the neighborhood of Delagoa Bay.

. . . Quite in a moment it seems, it is tomorrow—our last day in the tropics—and I go up on deck before the sun has risen, into the delicious moist warmth of the equatorial morning.

A man—a young man—is lounging in one of the bamboo chairs in a négligé of India silk—drinking a tiny cup of coffee and enjoying the early freshness. No one else is visible.

I hesitate a moment, conscious of the dishevelment of locks beneath the lace scarf tied under my chin, but think better of the hesitation and remain. I may never see this again, this world, where one is really for the first time

"Lord of the senses five,"

—where the light of night and of day have a new meaning; where one is drenched and steeped in color and perfume; where the husk of callous dulness falls away and every sense replies to impressions with a keenness as of new-born faculties.

. . . The young man's silky black head is ruffled too, and his yellow eyes still sleepy as he comes and leans over the rail. He is holding a little black pipe in a slim olive hand that is tipped with deep-tinted onyx-like nails, and with it he points to the first canoe putting out from shore. It is a long brown boat, very narrow, and filled with oranges heaped up in the centre.—It is cutting a delicate furrow along the pearly lilac of the glass-like sea.

A faint gray mist, scarcely more than a film, lies along the shore. Above it the red rocks stand up sharply against the white sky, which the coming sun is changing to gold.

The young man turns and smiles, showing a row of white teeth through lips as red as pomegranate flowers. He is English, but takes on here certain warm tones of color like a Spaniard.

Every moment I have spent in the tropics is to me just as vivid as this. I see everything. Not a beauty, not a touch of color, escapes me. Every moment of the day means intense delight, beauty, life. . . And now, after six months, not a line has faded or grown dim. I can live back in it in every emotion, every impression, as though not an hour divided me from it. . . It is well to have thus once really lived.

. . . The deck swarms with native merchants selling ostrich feathers, grass mats and baskets from Zanzibar; ornaments of shells, boxes of Turkish Delight, embroideries, photographs, and a three-months-old lion cub in a wooden cage.

The Bombay mail, for which we waited, has arrived, and new passengers come ashore with mountains of luggage. Among them is a man with a heavy, smooth, pink face, an overhanging upper lip and long white hair. It is Bradlaugh, the famous atheist, who fought the whole House of Commons, and forced it to admit him without taking the oath. He proves to be a jovial person, with an astounding ingenuity in misplacing h's, and an amusing little way of confiding small details concerning himself with an air of expecting you to snatch out a note-book and jot them down as one who should later make an article for one of the reviews, "Some Confidential Talks with Charles Bradlaugh, M.P." He is returning from India, where he has been attending a congress of natives agitating for representative government. His colleague, Sir William Wedderburn, returns with him—a Scotch baronet, a gentle enthusiast and theoretical radical, whose heart is overflowing with vague tenderness for all mankind.

There is some stir among us because Mr. Stanley has just arrived on the coast from the interior of Africa, and there is talk of his going home in our ship; but the government sends down a special convoy to take him to Egypt, and we steam away without him.

A cold west wind meets us in the Red Sea; the passengers get out their furs, and there is no more lounging on deck—one must walk briskly or sit in the sun wrapped in rugs.

I wake one night missing the throbbings of the screw, and find that we are going at a snail's pace in smooth water. The moon is very dim behind the clouds, and from the port-hole it would appear that we are sailing across endless expanses of sand: nothing else is to be seen. Morning shows a narrow ditch in a desert, half full of green water—so narrow and so shallow apparently that nothing would convince us our great ship could pass through save the actual proof of its doing so.

At one of the wider parts made for this purpose we pass a French troop-ship which dips her colors and sends a ringing cheer from the throats of the red-trousered soldiers on their way to Tonquin.

Later a dead Arab floats by in the green water, but is regarded with indifference as a common episode, and merely suggestive of an imprudent quarrel overnight.

Nothing is to be seen save stones and sand to the very horizon.

A dim and lurid sunset ends the day, and when night comes we are anchored off the town of Port Said—a wretched little place, dusty, dirty, and flaring with cheap vice—all the flotsam of four nations whirling about in an eddy of coarse pleasures. The shopkeepers are wolfish-looking, and bargain vociferously. Almost every other door opens into a gambling-hell and concert-hall. One of these gambling-places boasts an opera. At the tables stand amid the crowd two handsome young Germans—blond, but with none of the ruddy warmth of the English blond; pale and flaxen, with deep-blue eyes and haughty of manner. Not nice faces; high-bred, but cold and brutal. They are officers from Prince Henry of Prussia's ship, the Irene, lying now in the harbor.

In the concert-hall, "Traviata" is being sung by a fourth-rate French troupe, and the audience sit about at little tables, drinking, and eating ices. I ask for something native—Turkish—to drink, and they bring me a stuff that to all the evidences of sight, taste, and smell cries out that it is a mixture of paregoric and water, and one sip contents me. We are glad to go away.

ELIZABETH BISLAND

The Mediterranean is cold and not smooth, but here there comes upon one a sense of historical association.

In India nature is so tremendous she swallows up all memory of man; in Aden one remembers only the Bible; but nearing Greece the past takes shape and meaning, and history begins to have a new vividness and significance. Here man has been "lord of the visible earth"; has dominated and adorned her. She has been but the stage and background against which he played out the tragedies and comedies of humanity.

One morning at sunrise the stewardess taps at the door:

"The first officer's compliments, miss, and will you please get up and look out of the scuttle."

I wrap myself in my kimono—treasure-trove from Japan—and thrust head and shoulders through the wide port-hole. Directly before me is Candia—abrupt mountains rising sharply from the sea and crowned with snow. Among them are trailing clouds looping long scarfs of mist from peak to peak; at their feet Homer's "wine-dark sea," furrowed by a thousand keels: . . . Greek galleys, Roman triremes, fighting vessels from Carthage, merchant and battle ships from Venice, Genoa, and Turkey; the fleets of Spain; men-o'-war with the English lions at the peak; and, lastly, the world's peaceful commerce, sailing serenely over the bones and rotting hulls that lie below.

. . . The sun comes up gloriously out of the sea, deepening it to a winy purple in its light. Suddenly the mountain-tops take fire; the snow flushes softly, deepens rosily in hue, grows crimson with splendor; the sleeping mists begin to stir and heave, to lighten into gold, to float and rise into the warming blue above. Once more the splendors of a new day—such a sunrise as Cervantes may have seen; as glad Greek eyes may have witnessed bowing in prayer to the sun-god; as the galley-slave may have watched dully as a signal for new labors, and admirals gazed upon with tightening lip, not knowing whether the new sun should look upon defeat or victory, glory or death.

Then the dressing-gong clangs noisily through the ship and the colors pale into the common day.

Next morning, the 16th of January, we are fast to the docks at Brindisi, and but one more stage of the journey remains to be made.

Last Stage

I t is a vividly bright day in January, 1890—the 16th. There is a tingling crispness in the air as if it were early autumn—a slight frostiness that chills the skin, but does not penetrate the veins. Rather the deep breaths of this keen, pure sea ozone make the blood pulse with a swift, delicious warmth, like a plunge into cold water.

. . . We are anchored at Brindisi—the ancient Brundusium of the Romans—a town more than twenty-five centuries old, but which does not by any means look its age. It does not appear particularly attractive either from the wharves, and I am more than ever certain—as I always have been certain—that I could never agree with the haughty provincial who preferred to be first in Brundusium rather than second in Rome. Indeed, all efforts now are bent on being first out of Brundusium, as the train leaves within the hour. The Britannia goes on and around to Portsmouth, but the English government runs a train down through France and Italy to meet the P. and O. steamers, and thus gain five days in the arrival of the Indian and Australian mails. This mail train carries one passenger coach for the benefit of personages from the colonies who may be in haste to reach home; and if there are not a sufficient number of these distinguished servants of the empire to fill the car, more ordinary travellers can occupy the vacant berths by cabling ahead and securing them. I have taken this precaution at Ceylon, and find there will be no difficulty in the matter, provided I can get my luggage through the customs in time.

It is almost impossible to get anything done. The whole ship is in an uproar. Mails and luggage are being disembarked. Many passengers are leaving for a tour through Italy before finally returning to England, fearful of the winter fogs and of the influenza raging there. Italians, with cocked hats and imperial importance of manner, are bullying everyone and getting things into a hopeless tangle. My luggage is finally marked as passed; a porter is hired to transport it; I go off to attend to the visé of tickets, despatching of cables, and other minor matters, and arrive ten minutes before the advertised departure of the train.

. . . No luggage! I fling out of the car, rush back again to the ship, and discover the missing possessions in the hands of a pig-headed Italian who insists they have not been properly examined, and demands the keys.

Various necessary additions to my wardrobe during the voyage have so enlarged the contents of my little box that only careful packing and the emphatic sitting down upon it of the stewardess and myself have induced it to shut at all. Now this amiable official insists, despite the fact that it goes under seal and bond straight through to England, upon opening it and strewing my garments about the deck.

I hope I did not forget the dignity a gentlewoman should preserve under the most trying of circumstances, but I fancy that my tones, while low, were concentrated, and that the little American I used was "frequent and fluent and free," for the man turned pale and wavered.

I snatched up my belongings, flung them in pell-mell, jumped upon the box, snapped to the hasp, and ran off with a porter towards the train, blank despair in my heart. Happily, Italian trains are not bound down by narrow interpretations of time-tables, and I do succeed in catching it, with the luggage and some few tattered remnants of a once nice temper.

It is very destructive of the mental equilibrium to lose the temper so thoroughly, especially if one is out of practice, and it is fully an hour before the exceeding beauty of the country through which we are passing begins to have its soothing effect and to make me fain to forgive the Italians because of Italy! On our right is the Adriatic, blue as lapis-lazuli and gay with flocking sails. Here and there lie little snow-white towns along its shores, and between are the gray olive orchards, that have something strangely human in their gnarled grotesqueness. Even in flying by one sees flashes of fantastic gargoyle-like resemblances to persons one has known, caricatured into impossible contortions, as if by some mediæval humorousness. It is not difficult to comprehend how people who lived among olive groves developed dryad superstitions and created legends of flying women transformed into trees.

... The English government pays the Italian government a large subsidy for this train and the swift passage of the mails, but the ubiquitous person who attends to all our needs—is porter, guard, steward, cook, and brakeman in one—has his own ideas on the subject of haste, and acts accordingly. When we reach a town where he has friends he goes out, quietly winds us up like a Waterbury watch, dismounts, and is received with affectionate enthusiasm by a little crowd on the platform. He inquires solicitously after each one's kin unto the fourth and fifth generation, gives his careful attention to all the local gossip, and retails the news he has been gathering all along the line. When he can no longer hear or tell some new thing he remembers our existence, climbs once more upon his perch, lets us run down with a sudden whir, and we go on our way. At mealtimes he retires into a tiny den amidships, and from a space but little larger than a match-box produces delightful soups and salads, excellent coffee, well-cooked game, baskets of twisted Italian bread; wine and oranges. At night he arranges our sleeping-berths, and I think would perform barber duties and assist with our toilets if called upon to do so. He is a fatigued and blasé personage who looks as if chronically deprived of his due allowance of sleep, and he evidently regards the travelling public as a helpless, nervous creature always in a peevishly ridiculous hurry.

We begin to climb into the mountains, and it grows very cold. Oddly-angled vineyards hang precariously to the steep sides of the heights, propped into place by dams of stone that keep the soil from sliding down hill. Queer villages are tucked into clefts, with streets that are merely narrow stairs. Now and again we flash by the bold outlines of a ruined castle crowning a crag: the site always chosen with so much discretion that one wonders not only how enemies ever got in, but how the owners themselves ever emerged—unless they fell out.

. . . A film of snow appears here and there, and the cold intensifies. Suddenly we catch a glimpse of white heights outlined against the blue—we are among the Alps, and the Mount Cenis tunnel is not far away.

. . . A space of darkness, of thundering, clattering echoes—and then France!

. . . Everything is quite different all at once. A fine new fortress commands the tunnel; the station is better built, larger, and in better repair than those we have seen in Italy. The customs officer, a well-set-up and good-looking Frenchman in a smart uniform, inquires politely if we have anything to declare, and when we answer in the negative sets his heels together, gives a profound salutation, and vexes us no more.

Everywhere is an air of greater prosperity, thrift, and alertness. The train does not stop to admit of gossiping, and goes at added speed.

Telegrams have been following me along the route concerning the possibility of catching a ship at Havre. The train is rather behind time, and unless the Transatlantique will consent to delay her departure for an hour or two, it will be useless to attempt to cover the space between Villeneuve, Paris, and Havre before tomorrow at seven. There is hope, however, that she will wait, and Friday night, some two hours after midnight, the guard rouses me to deliver a telegram which says I must be ready at four to change cars for Paris. This means leaving my box—it is under seal for London—and crossing the ocean with the few belongings in a travelling-bag. I rise and dress quietly, scribble a few notes of farewell to such of my fellow passengers as have been especially courteous, and am all ready when we halt at Villeneuve. A young Frenchman, agent for Cook's tourist bureau in Paris, has come to meet me, but brings the discouraging intelligence that the ship has refused to wait and that there is no chance of catching her. It is not until reaching America that I discover this is a mistake and that the Transatlantique waited several hours, not only in the harbor, but when the tide made it necessary to cross the bar, lingering outside for another half-hour in hopes I might still come, for the French captain was interested in my endeavor, and had received official permission for the delay.

This change subjected me to inconvenience and to suffering, from the effects of which it took much time to entirely recover. For then began a most trying experience, from the strain of which not even the most vigorous constitution could escape unharmed. The cause of this false information was never satisfactorily ascertained. It, however, succeeded in lengthening the voyage four days.

. . . It is too late—half-past four—to return to bed, so I throw myself on the couch and wait for day. A faint rime clouds the window when dawn breaks, but a breath dispels it, and outside are lovely Corot-like visions—pale, shadowy, gray—worth the lost sleep to have seen. Here and there a thin plume of smoke curls up against the dull frosty sky from the chimney of a thatched, lime-washed cottage set amid barns and stacks.

As the day grows peasants such as Millet pictures come out of the cottages and follow the road, carrying fagots or baskets of potatoes and turnips.

Two legs and a pair of sabots appear under a perambulating heap of hay.

A big dog drags a small cart full of milk-cans, and a woman with a cap and tucked-up skirts trudges along beside, blowing on her fingers to warm them.

All this, just as did Italy, seems very familiar. I know it quite well from pictures and books. It gives one the sensation—reversed—awakened by reading a realistic novel in which all the little details of daily life are minutely and accurately reproduced.

It is ten o'clock when we reach Calais, and the Dover boat has gone, so there is time for a bath and breakfast—luckily, as I shall not have another meal for forty-eight hours; but of this I have no prevision.

The Channel is gray and stormy when we start, and a gout of rain splashes now and then upon the deck. Fat old French gentlemen spread themselves out in *chaises longues* and make all necessary preparations for sea-sickness. The English turn up the collars of their long coats, thrust their hands in the pockets, and stride along the rolling deck. Later the sun struggles through the clouds and turns the gloom to a stormy gray-green and shifting silver—and there looms slowly through the mists the white cliffs of England!

For me this keen windy sea is thick with phantom sails: . . . the high-beaked galleys of the Conqueror, the silken wings of the White Ship, Henry's fleet carrying victorious armies into France, Drake's and Raleigh's prows, galleons from the East, certain small sailing craft going swiftly and furtively by dusk, carrying fugitive monarchs—the myriad wings of a nation of sea-birds, spread for pleasure or for prey. . .

Starting two months ago from a vast continent which the English race have made their own, where the English tongue, English laws, customs, and manners reign from sea to sea, in my whole course around the globe I have heard that same tongue, seen the same laws and manners, found the same race. Have had proof with my own eyes of the splendor of their empire, of their power, their wealth, of their dominance and orgulousness, of their superb armies, their undreamable commerce, their magnificent possessions, their own unrivalled physical beauty and force—and lo! now at last I find from a tiny island ringed with gray seas has sprung this race of kings. It fills my soul with a passion of pride that I, too, am an Anglo-Saxon. In my veins, too, runs that virile tide that pulses through the heart of this Lord of the Earth—the blood of this clean, fair, noble English race! . . .

It is worth a journey round the world to see—

> "This royal throne of kings, this sceptred isle,
> This earth of majesty, this seat of Mars,
> This other Eden, demi-paradise;
> This fortress built by nature for herself
> Against infestion and the hand of war.
> This happy breed of men, this little world;
> This precious stone set in a silver sea;
> This blessed plot of earth, this realm, this England,
> This nurse, this teeming womb of royal kings,
> Feared by their breed and famous by their birth,

Renownèd for their deeds so far from home,
For Christian service and true chivalry,
This land of such dear souls, this dear, dear land—
England, bound in with the triumphant sea!"

—and I understand now the meaning of this trumpet-cry of love and pride from the greatest of earth's poets—an Englishman.

. . . Dover—and one sets foot at last on the mother soil. (We are, by the way, the only people who call our land a mother.)

. . . the blue boudoir of a first-class carriage—then English landscapes under the level rays of a setting sun.

Certain characteristics here are very reminiscent of Japan. The neatness and completeness of everything; the due allowance of trees dispersed in ornamental fashion; nature so thoroughly tamed and domesticated; the picturesque railway stations, and a certain moist softness in the air. But where everything there is light, fragile, and fantastic, here it is solid, compact, and durable.

. . . Like the English sea, the English land swarms with phantoms— the folk of history, of romance, of poetry and fiction. They troop along the roads, prick across the fields, look over the hedges, and peer from every window. I hear the clang of their armor, see the waving of their banners; their voices ring in the frosty winter air, their horses' hoof-beats sound along the paths. Without regard to time or period, to reality or non-reality, they come in hosts to welcome me—to say, "And so you, too, have come to join us. We have waked to greet you. We are the ghosts of England's past!"

Even the folk of the contemporary fiction have not failed to be present. I see the sunk fence by the coppice where Angelina always bids Edwin an eternal farewell in the last chapter of the second volume, and they are there doing it now. There rides Captain Cavendish in his red coat, home from the hunting-field, and on his way to the handsome old country-house yonder where he will squeeze Mrs. Fitzroy's fingers under the teacup he passes her and thus lay the foundation for forty-two chapters of jealously, hatred, and all uncharitableness.

. . . Darkness falls. A dull glare is reflected from the heavens that speaks the presence of a great gas-lit city. A myriad sparks twinkle in the distance—the "Lights o' London!"

. . . Miles and miles and miles of houses. A huge, shadowy half-globe looming against the sky—the dome of St. Paul's.

. . . towers and delicate spires, and lights shining through many lance-like windows—Parliament Houses, where lords and commons sit in debate.

. . . long gleams quivering serpent-like across a wavering black flood—we have passed over the Thames, and here is Charing Cross.

. . . Clatter, hurry, and confusion—everyone giving different suggestions and directions. I had meant to remain overnight in London and take the North-German Lloyd steamer at Southampton the next day, but here the news meets me that this ship has been suddenly withdrawn and will not sail till late in the week. My one chance is the night mail to Holyhead and to catch the Bothnia, which touches at Queenstown next morning. This train leaves in an hour and a half. I have not slept since two o'clock the night before, nor eaten since breakfast, and my courage is nearly at an end. One of my fellow-travellers, who has been most kind to me all the way from Ceylon, comes to my rescue and assumes all responsibilities. I am sent off to the hotel to dine in company with two kind and charming fellow-voyagers, Sir William Lewis and his daughter, while he arranges my difficulties. I am far too tired and disturbed, however, to eat, and can only crumble my bread and taste my wine. At half-past eight my friend appears and carries me off to the Euston station. He has snatched his dinner, got rid of the dust of travel, and into evening clothes. He has brought rugs and cushions that I may have some rest during the night, a little cake in case I grow hungry, and heaps of books and papers. My foot-warmer is filled with hot water, the guard is induced to give me his best care and attention, and then I go away alone again, somewhat comforted by the chivalrous goodness of the travelling man to the uncared-for woman.

. . . I fall asleep from fatigue, am shaken by horrible dreams, and start awake with a cry. The train is thundering through a wild storm. I try to read, but the words dance up and down the page. The guard comes now and then to see if I need anything, and deep in the night I reach Holyhead. Gathering up my multitudinous belongings, I run through the rain and sleet to the little vessel quivering and straining at the pier. The night is a wild one, the wind in our teeth, and the journey rough and very tedious. The cold and tempestuous day has dawned before we touch Kingstown and are hurried—wretched for lack of sleep and the means of making a fresh toilet—into the train for Dublin. The Irish capital is still unawake when I rattle across it from station to station this Sunday morning, and immediately I am off again at full speed through a land swept with flying mists and showers—a beautiful land, green even in January.

Later I see ruddy-cheeked peasants going along the roads to church—a type I am familiar with in America. I gaze contemplatively at these sturdy young men, and wonder how soon they will be New York aldermen and mayors of Chicago; how soon those rosy girls, in their queer, bunchy, provincial gowns, will be leaders of society in Washington and dressed by Worth.

. . . I am growing frightfully hungry, having eaten nothing since yesterday morning in Calais. There is the spice cake, but with no liquid save a little brandy in a flask, I soon choke upon the cake and abandon it. The train is behind time, owing to the late arrival of the Channel boat, and stops only for the briefest moments. At noon we reach Queenstown, having curved around a fair space of water and past the beautiful city of Cork. The ship has not yet arrived, but will doubtless be here in a few moments, the bad weather having delayed her; and my luggage is all hurried down to the tender, where I should be sent, too, did I not wail with hunger. The Queen's Hotel is not far from the station, but the evil luck which has pursued me for the last two days ordains that the kitchen of this hostelry should be undergoing repairs at this particular moment, and no food is to be had. By dint of perseverance, in frantic protest and reckless objurgation, I finally secure a cup of rather cold and bitter tea and a bit of dingy bread that looks as if it had been used to scrub the floor with before being presented to me as a substitute for breakfast. I am warned to hold myself in readiness for an instantaneous summons to the tender, for when the steamer is signalled there is no time to waste. So hastily I make such toilet as is possible with my dressing-bag aboard the tender, and sit alone in the waiting-room attendant on the summons.

Hour after hour goes by, but no summons comes. I dare not move lest the call come during my absence, and sit there hopeless, helpless, overwhelmed with hunger, lack of sleep, and fatigue. At six o'clock my patience is at end, and I am clamorously demanding more food, when they bring the long-expected notice. The ship has been signaled, and the tender must be off.

It rains in torrents, mingled with sleet, and the wind blows a tempest. The tender puts out from shore and is whirled about like an eggshell. The wind drives us back, and over and over again we essay the passage before we can make head against the wild weather. It is two hours and a half later when we get alongside the ship, and I am chilled to the bone, sick and dizzy for want of food and sleep, and climb stumblingly across the narrow, slippery, plunging path that leads from one ship to the other. No sooner have I set foot on the glassy deck than the push of an impatient passenger sends me with a smashing fall into the scuppers, where I gather bruises that last a week. A compassionate stewardess comes to the rescue and puts me to bed—speechless and on the verge of tears.

. . . The weather is terrible—a season long to be remembered for the January storms of the north Atlantic. The waves toss our ship back and forth among them like a football. Even were I not too miserable to move, the plunging of the vessel would make it impossible to keep one's feet. The ship laboriously climbs a howling green mountain, pauses irresolute a moment on the crest, and then toboggans madly down the farther side, her screw out of water, and kicking both heels madly in the air to the utter dislocation of one's every tooth and joint. Down, down she goes, as if boring for bottom, and when it is perfectly certain that she can never by any chance right herself, she comes nose upmost with a jerk, shakes off the water, and attack a new mountain, to repeat the same performance on the farther side.

Two thirds of the passengers are very seasick, and I quite as wretched and prostrate from my late painful experiences as if still subject to the malady. It is the third or fourth day out, and I am beginning to take heart of grace and to long to leave my stuffy little cabin. The ship is rolling frightfully still, and while revolving in my mind an attempt to rise, a sudden lurch sends the heavy jug full of water flying out of its basin into the berth, where it smashes into twenty pieces upon my face and chest, and drenches me with icy water. The doors of the gangway are left open lest they freeze together, and therefore a bitter wind sweeps through the cabin, so that when hauled from my dripping bed, and it is discovered that the key of my box, where are the only dry changes of garment, is mislaid, I am stabbed through and through my wet and clinging clothes by this terrible cold. Thus suppressed again for another three days, it is only towards the end of the week—the storm being abated—that I am able once more to stand on my feet. It is a most amiable and friendly little company that finally assembles in the cabin; the recent woes we have all passed through having made us sympathetic and considerate. We even get up in time a concert for the seamen's orphans, and play shuffle-board on the still uncertain deck for prizes. But this crossing of the zone of storms has greatly delayed us, and it is late in the evening of the eleventh day when we take our pilot aboard. The morning of the twelfth day is cold, but evidently has some thought of clearing, and the sea is less rough.

. . . A rim of opaque film grows on the horizon that the emigrants on the forward deck regard with eager interest and hope. The passengers stand about in furs, pinched and shivering; their noses red, but their eyes full of pleased anticipation. Any land would be dear and desirable after near a fortnight of this cold and frantic sea—but when it is one's own—!

The film thickens and darkens, and suddenly resolves itself into Coney Island, where, as we swiftly near the shore, the plaintive reproachful eyes of the great wooden elephant are turned upon us as if to deprecate our late coming.

The water has smoothed itself into a bay, and a huge gray woman, holding an uplifted torch, awaits our coming; the emigrants regard her wonderingly—the symbol of liberty held aloft, and a benignant countenance turned towards all the outer world. We are by the shores of Staten Island. A pretty English girl who has braved the winter storms to follow her new husband to a foreign country remarks surprisedly that all this looks much like England—evidently having expected log-cabins and a country town. But I have no time to be amused at her ignorance—I am saying joyously to myself

> "Is this the hill, is this the kirk,
> Is this mine ain countree?"

Suddenly a great flood of familiarity washes away the memory of the strange lands and people I have seen and blots out all sense of time that has elapsed since I last saw all this. I know how everything—the streets, the houses, the passers-by—are looking at this moment. It is as if I had turned away my head for an instant, and now looked back again. My duties, my cares, my interests, which had grown dim and shadowy in these last two months, suddenly take on sharp outlines and become alive and real once more. I feel as if I had but sailed down the bay for an hour, and was now returning.

. . . The ship slides into dock. I can see the glad faces of my friends upon the pier. My journey is done. I have been around the world in seventy-six days.

THE END

A Note About the Author

Elizabeth Bisland (1861–1929) was an American journalist, editor, and travel writer. Born in Louisiana, Bisland fled her homestead with her family during the Civil War, later settling in Natchez. As a teenager, she began publishing poems in the *New Orleans Times Democrat*, which would soon offer her a job. In 1887, Bisland moved to New York City, where she found work with *The Sun* and *The New York World*, eventually taking a position as an editor with then-fledgling magazine *Cosmopolitan*. Her break came in 1889, when she was sent on assignment to compete with Nellie Bly—who worked for the *New York World*—on her journey around the globe. Although both women departed from Manhattan on the same day, and despite the press generated by their competition, Bly remains more widely recognized for her role in the stunt. Upon returning, Bisland published her account of the adventure as *In Seven Stages: A Flying Trap Around the World* (1891).

A Note from the Publisher

Spanning many genres, from non-fiction essays to literature classics to children's books and lyric poetry, Mint Edition books showcase the master works of our time in a modern new package. The text is freshly typeset, is clean and easy to read, and features a new note about the author in each volume. Many books also include exclusive new introductory material. Every book boasts a striking new cover, which makes it as appropriate for collecting as it is for gift giving. Mint Edition books are only printed when a reader orders them, so natural resources are not wasted. We're proud that our books are never manufactured in excess and exist only in the exact quantity they need to be read and enjoyed.

bookfinity™

Discover more of your favorite classics with Bookfinity™.

- Track your reading with custom book lists.
- Get great book recommendations for your personalized Reader Type.
- Add reviews for your favorite books.
- AND MUCH MORE!

Visit **bookfinity.com** and take the fun Reader Type quiz to get started.

Enjoy our classic and modern companion pairings!

Classic & Modern

* 9 7 8 1 5 1 3 2 9 2 2 3 6 *